Mo'orea island Travel and Tourism

Tour and Vacation.

Author

Adam Evans

Publisher

by

James-Cloude Printing .

Rue 34 Face Canary Maroc Anador

Youpougon Cote d'Ivoire

Table of Content

Introduction

The Magical Island

A few minutes from the island of Tahiti by plane, and only thirty minutes by high-speed catamaran, Moorea soars magically out of the ocean in an explosion of green velvet - what you would imagine a South Seas island to be.

A wide, shallow lagoon surrounds the island's vertical mountains where poetic threads of waterfalls tumble down fern-softened cliffs. Peaceful meadows flanked by pinnacles of green will fill your senses and renew your belief in the majesty of nature. Pastel-painted houses surrounded by gardens of hibiscus and birds of paradise, circle the island in a fantasy of happy, yet simple villages.

A favourite among repeat visitors who all agree!!!

The beauty of Moorea is unforgettable.!!!

Aimeo I Te Rara Varu

This, the island's poetic name, comes from the eight majestic mountain ridges; however, the name was later changed to Moorea-meaning "Yellow lizard"-following a dream by a high priest.

Polynesian legend describes the panorama of volcanic ridges as the second dorsal fin of the fish that became the island of Tahiti. These pinnacles later inspired the mythical "Bali Hai" that was based on James Michener's book, Tales of the South Pacific.

About Moorea

Moorea is Tahiti's less-populous and smaller neighbor, the second island in the Windward group of Society Islands. Though close in proximity to Tahiti and sharing much of the natural beauty, Moorea nonetheless retains a distinct identity. In the pre-contact period the island had a vibrant population and at times dominated its larger neighbor.

Central to this population was the Opunohu Valley in Moorea, still filled with archaeological sites and with many excavations and reconstructions of old structures. The sites are rich with information about population distribution, religious practices, and social stratification. Roger C. Green studied the archaeological remains in the 1960s and found the Opunohu Valley to be an important center of the island's culture. Further, the number and type of the structures located in this valley suggest that Moorea was an important center of culture and religion across the Society Islands.

The subsequrent archaeological exploration of this center has significantly changed our perceptions of pre-contact Moorean society. The prevailing thought had been that the ari'i and ra'atira, the chiefs and people of higher rank, lived on the coasts while the manahume lived further inland. The presence of important architecture such as marae in the interior debunked this theory, as it showed that there were people of higher status living further inland. This has changed our understanding of the traditional relationships between the ari'i, ra'atira, and manahune, and it also furthered understanding of land distribution customs.

Green found agricultural terraces, residential areas, religious structures, specialized structures, and "functionally unassigned constructions when he came to Moorea. Mooreans mainly built stone structures, and used untouched or shaped stones in their constructions. Their mastery of stonework is evident, and even today the surviving stone structures used for many generations evoke a sense of permanence.

The religious structures were of particular importance to anthropologist Jennifer Kahn, who studied them in 2010 in a larger investigation of the cult of 'Oro, a very powerful religious sect at the time of the European contact. She wanted "to highlight what archaeological studies can tell us about 'Oro style temples and their place in late prehistoric sociopolitical transformations in the Society Islands," and to reveal the effects that the worship of 'Oro had on the politics and society of Moorea. She used Moorea as a case study to understand larger themes within the Society Islands.

The temples were built by the ari'i (nobility) and were used by chiefs to politically legitimize themselves and show their domination. Building a marae required manpower, material, and power, so by building these marae and claiming ownership of them, the ari'i and ari'i rahi were asserting their strength and godliness. The temples were made with rounded stones meant to symbolize turtle heads, which could be substituted for human offerings in some Eastern Polynesian societies. Manipulating stones into this shape requires massive amounts of labor, further asserting the influence of the people building the temple. This type of building using rounded stones was unique to Tahiti and Moorea.

The newly excavated inland marae suggest that the chiefs were building these structures to show loyalty to the 'Oro war cult, and by extension to the Tahitian Pomare lineage. The building of temples served both a religious and political function. Because Moorea and Tahiti are so close, interactions between the two islands were frequent, and the ari'i wanted to align themselves with the powerful clans on Tahiti.

Although many of these sites have already been excavated and studied, there is still more information to be obtained from them. These sites can be used to establish the date of the introduction of the cult of 'Oro to the Society Islands, but dating has yet to be performed with modern techniques. Though archaeologists have been studying Moorea for a long time, much of the early studies were colored by presumptions based on previous Western images of the island.

The journals of missionaries and explorers provide substantial and important firsthand accounts, although since their views are decidedly one-sided, it is crucial to view these sources with a critical eye. Captain James Cook visited Moorea on his third voyage, and detailed his experiences with the inhabitants of the island in his journal. One of Cook's objectives was to observe and record the lands and peoples with whom he came into contact. The presence of his ships created a stir among the people and consequently made it difficult for him to record the people in their "normal" state; furthermore, as a captain, he tended to interact with the higher chiefs of the society, rather than the manahune, or commoners.

Admiral William Waldegrave, captain of HMS Seringapatam, visited Moorea in 1830. Waldegrave arrived with preconvceived notions of Moorean "savages," and adjusted his experiences to his previous perceptions of islanders rather than the other way around. He described Moorean resources and workers in terms of an already developing global economy.

"These islands could produce anything that will grow within the tropics, but until a change takes place in the habits and dispositions of the people, no trade can thrive," he observed, further noting that earlier missionaries, who had attempted to set up a cotton farm could not coerce the natives to work on it.] Waldegrave also commented on the morals and sexual habits of the natives, whose "lasciviousness" he found "disgusting." Observing a decline in population compared to the estimate of Cook in the late-eighteenth century, Waldgrave placed the blame not on introduced European diseases but on non-European practices. "The vices of the people were such that nothing but the abandonment of Paganism, and the conversion to Christianity, could have saved" the remaining population, he lamented, later specifically referencing apparently widely practiced infanticide as the apparent cause of the losses. Waldegrave applied his European moral and social system to a distant people who developed in a different time and place from his own, and was unsuccesful at assimilating the disparate culture into his worldview.

In 1890, the artist John LaFarge and his good friend Henry Adams traveled to the Moorea, enticed by the pervading image of Polynesia as a tropical paradise. Adams wrote, "in thus imitating Robert Louis Stephenson[sic] I am inspired by no wish for fame or future literary or political notoriety, or even by motives of health, but merely by a longing to try something new and different." Likewise, LaFarge felt the influence of the past Europeans when visiting the island. On Moorea he wrote: "

My impressions of to-day become confused and connected with these old printed records of the last century, until I seem to be treading the very turf that the first discoverers walked on, and to be shaded by the trees." The legacy of the people that came before him, such as Cook, Herman Melville, and Stevenson, drew these men to the South Seas, and their presence was felt by both of them throughout their journey. The South Seas held a special allure to artists and writers. A few years after LaFarge and Adams visited, Paul Gauguin traveled to Polynesia. Gauguin was drawn by the same idea of an untouched land and culture whose inhabitants lived as "noble savages." For LaFarge, the innate natural beauty of the island, free from the corrupting influence of people and the West, was captivating.

LaFarge's first sight of Moorea was from Tahiti. He describes the view, saying "It made an enchanted vision of peaks and high mountains, as strange as any which you may have seen in the backgrounds of old Italian paintings, far enough to be vague in the twilight haze and yet distinct in places high up, where the singular shapes were modeled in pink and yellow-green." La Farge was primarily a landscape painter,

11

and it was the landscape of Moorea that captured his imagination. Adams, though not a painter, was also captivated by Moorea's physical beauty, describing his arrival at an island, where "the mountains, in peaks and with outlines as unreasonable as a theatre drop-scene, rose around us, more like the Lake of Como than like a respectable Polynesian island. The scene was impressive: the finest we have yet struck."

Several of his LaFarge's paintings of Moorea are as viewed from Tahiti. Its untouched nature and physical beauty, in contrast to the hustle and bustle of Papeete, is a powerful image. When he actually arrived on the island, LaFarge continued to paint landscapes, but in a different fashion. He usually did studies of particular views, painting the same image or place in different times of day to see how it changed, and he did this on Moorea with the peak of Maua Roa. The changes in weather, perspective and time of day all interested

LaFarge, and the peak of this mountain anchored his studies of the island.

Many of his other paintings from this trip depict the people of the islands dancing, or going about their lives, but there are no paintings of the people of Moorea. The physical beauty of the island, not its culture or people, was the primary attraction for LaFarge. His primary medium is watercolors, which gives images of the island a dreamlike, unreal quality.

LaFarge and Adams, artist and writer, provide a European view of the island of Moorea, typical of their time. Moorea was (and is) a physically beautiful place, its disengagement from the busy island of Tahiti holding, then as now, the most allure. Whether by taking a scientific study of the structures and ruins there, or by putting the beauty of the island down in paintings, there have been many attempts to understand the island and its landscape.

Much of the modern documentation available on Moorea focuses on tourism, particularly in popular media such as newspapers and websites. 46 of the first 50 websites one finds on a Google search of Moorea are advertisements for hotel rooms or other tourist packages, or blog entries describing one's tourist experience.

Additionally, coverage of Moorea in major newspapers in the US such as the New York Times and the Los Angeles Times is limited to the travel section the former's "Moorea's Sumptuous Sands" is one of the only feature articles on record of the island, while the latter's coverage of Moorea is limited to "World's Most Romantic Places to Propose."[18]   Because there is such a dearth of information on Moorea outside of these few portrayals, one gets the idea that Moorea is something of a tourist hotspot.

However, in reality, tourism is a much less significant part of the island's life than one would gather. Moorea has no obvious urban center, or even a true central village; it has no gift shops or markets and few restaurants or even stores, and the tourist that leaves the hotel finds little that caters to his interests. Upon arriving on Moorea one finds beautiful but rubbly coral beaches, small-scale agriculture producing mainly tropical fruits such as pineapple, scattered horse ranches and a good deal of jungle. While tourism is a feature of the landscape as well there is at least one five-star hotel, a Sheraton, and the few shops and restaurants that exist are happy to serve visitors it is clear that this is not an economy or society dominated by tourism the way many tourist spots are.

Another prominent feature of the island community is marine research, as two major research stations, the University of California at Berkeley's Gump Station and the French national laboratory, are located on island.

Moorea is a valuable island for researchers, as geologically it is in the process of transitioning from a high island to a coral atoll, meaning that the island itself is eroding while the surrounding reefs develop. The publications of these centers provide another significant source of documentation, and are invaluable for those studying coral reef ecology. However, this also creates an overly large perception of the importance of marine research for the islanders themselves.

The Gump Station contributes a good deal of funding to community projects, including co-sponsoring the building of a Polynesian cultural center known as the Atitia Center on its property on island.[19] UCB students and faculty have also presented their work to students at the Oponohu High School, a local agricultural trade school attracting students from across French Polynesia. The Gump Station and its students and faculty are an important part of the island community; however, it should be noted that the research itself is conducted by non-native, often temporary residents, and that academic research is not a common occupation for Moorean islanders themselves.

In endeavoring to capture Moorea, many authors have been colored by their individual biases and have ultimately failed to paint a complete picture of the island. While tourism and marine research are important to the island's economy, focusing exclusively on these overshadows the daily lives of islanders, many of whom work in subsistence agriculture or commute to Tahiti. Similarly, to read historical accounts is often to read of colonization attempts or missionary work, which tends not to capture the islanders' perspective. The end result for the reader is often an outsider's portrait of the island, a collection of foreign opinions about an island that has a culture of its own.

Adam Evans

Moorea Physical Environment

Located in the remote South Pacific, the island of Moorea is one of the world's most beautiful landscapes as well as one of the region's most well studied physical environments. Moorea is part of a chain of islands formed by hot spot volcanism; once an underwater volcano forms the island, it begins to erode and sink back into the ocean, meaning these islands are constantly changing. Moorea is in the beginning stages of transformation from a high island to a coral atoll, a geologic transition that has a profound effect on the island's physical environment.

The island is home to two major research stations: The University of California at Berkley's Gump Station and the French National Centre for Scientific Research's Centre de Reherches Insulaires et Observatoire de l'Environnenment (Le CROIBE). Both stations are focused on studying the reef system of the island, which is an ecosystem that has both economic and intrinsic value to the local population. This stage of transition, extensive academic research, and the reef's value as a human resource make the island an important site for potential conservation.

Moorea is the second largest island in the Society Archipelago, located in the Southern Equatorial Pacific Ocean. It is roughly twenty km northwest of Tahiti, the largest island, and is a member of the Windward group. Moorea is a high island, making it rugged and mountainous with fertile soils and several watersheds ("Moorea," Encyclopedia Britannica). Of forty-six watersheds, the two most dominant are the Pao Pao and Opunohi river valleys on the northern edge of the island (Duane 2).

The watersheds flow from several small peaks on the island, the highest of which is Mount Tohivea at 1,207 m high ("Moorea," Encyclopedia Britannica). These small mountains slowly descend to the coastline, ninety percent of which is lined by offshore barrier reefs. Twelve deep navigable passes separate the reefs and allow access for mariners (Duane 2). The lagoon, an important element of Moorea's transition from high volcanic island to coral atoll, is an economic resource for both fishing and tourism (gomoorea.com).

The process of hot spot volcanism that formed the island defines Moorea's geology. Studies on the age of rocks in Moorea have concluded the dormant volcano that is the island was active between 1.2 and 2.6 million years ago (Dymond 236). These dates indicate that Moorea is in the early stages of the process of transformation from a high island to an atoll, a metamorphosis that can be easily visualized by observing Moorea's significant coral reef, volcanic mountains, and substantial lagoon.

Moorea's lush vegetation is one of the qualities that gives the island its beautiful tropical appearance. However, the island's vegetation has changed dramatically as human inhabitants shaped it for their uses. The first Polynesians traveled to Moorea as early as 1200 years ago, bringing with them breadfruit, chestnut, taro, and medicinal species to ensure their survival (Eichenseher). Later, European explorers brought plants from their gardens, including many medicinal and ornamental species. One such species, the ornamental Miconia calvescens--commonly called miconia--has become one of the South Pacific's most dangerous invasive species. Aggressive invasives like miconia, threaten to overwhelm the islands' few endemic species as well as introduced species that have value to the islands' people (Meyer and Florence).

The climate of Moorea, similar to the other islands of French Polynesia, is tropical with a mean annual temperature of 26°C (Male). Moorea experiences a rainy season between December and February, when most of the annual 109 inches of precipitation fall, as well as a dry season between March and November (Male, Duane 3). The rainy season, with an average temperature of 26.5°C, is slightly warmer than the wet season, with an average temperature of 24.5°C, though temperatures are moderate all year (Duane 2).

The prevailing winds in Moorea are the easterly trade winds, which fuel the island's dominant current the South Equatorial Current (Segar 242). Easterly trade winds and easterly current are consistent through most of the year. During normal years, the easterly trade winds, which bring warm air to the Western Pacific, make Moorea's location in the central ocean relatively safe from cyclones. However, this pattern is reversed in El Niño years when westerly winds carry warm air to the central Pacific, making Moorea and other French Polynesian islands vulnerable to cyclones (Meteo France). The extreme variability in storm frequency can make El Niño years dangerous in French Polynesia, whose population may be unprepared for violent and frequent hurricanes.

An important feature of Moorea's physical environment is the developing coral reef. Corals, like anemones and jellyfish, are members of the phylum Cnidarians. Corals are tube-like structures with a central cavity and a mouth surrounded by tentacles (CRC Reef Research Centre). Coral reefs are formed when free-swimming larvae attach to hard surfaces along the edge of islands or continents ("What are Corals?"). Moorea's reef is dominated by four genera: Porities, Pocillopora, Acropora, and Montipora (Gump

Station, 5). Once the corals grow vertically to sea level, the colonies then expand horizontally. An indicator of the beginning of high island transformation is the development of a reef. As Moorea ages, the growth of the reef will reflect the progression in transformation.

Currently, the developing reef of Moorea is an offshore barrier reef (Gump Station, 3). This reef system creates a series of shallow and narrow channels ranging from five to seven meters in depth and one to one-and-a-half kilometers in width (Gump Station, 3). On the north shore of the island there is a particularly dense section of reef that contains about fifty percent of the coral around Moorea (Gump Station, 4). Moorea's reef is relatively pristine and undisturbed and is home to an abundance of reef fish and corals that are high in diversity, indicating the robust condition of the ecosystem (Gump Station, 4).

The impact of human activity on the reef is substantial, and the most prominent threats in Moorea stem from fishing, pollution, and climate disruption. Some fishing methods leave reefs polluted and damaged ("Anthropogenic Threats to Corals"). In addition, overfishing has reduced the number of top predators in Moorea's reef, which has led to degradation of the trophic cascade (Gump Station, 5). When top predators are removed from the food chain, prey species populations can become large due to a lack of regulation through predation. Increased populations of these prey species changes the demands on the reef environment. Ironically, the lack of predators combined with the relatively low-pressure subsistence fishing by the human population means reef fish populations remain diverse and abundant. Even though the ecosystem appears to be in balance, the lack of top predators represents a regrettable loss of diversity in this unique environment.

Marine pollution is a threat that can occur through coastal development, agriculture, and land based runoff. All of these factors introduce some type of sediment, nutrient, chemical, insecticide, oil, or debris that is foreign to the reef environment ("Anthropogenic Threats to Corals"). Moorea's volcanic soils are very productive, and agriculture on Moorea includes the cultivation of products such as vanilla, copra, and even coffee ("Moorea," Encyclopedia Britannica). Additional development on Moorea could limit reef productivity by introducing extensive runoff to the lagoon or barrier reef (Duane).

Climate disruption is a global problem and its effect on coral reefs is significant. Consequences of climate disruption, such as increased sea surface temperature, ocean acidification, and increased sea level all create change in the coral environment (Gump Station, 5). Ocean acidification and increasing sea surface temperature affect the rate of calcification and therefore the rate of growth for corals (Gump Station, 5). Temperature especially affects the mutualistic relationship between the zooxanthellae and coral, which can cause coral bleaching (Gump Station, 5). The Gump station's ecological study was unable to detect damage to the reef as a result of climate disruption thus far. However, additional monitoring is important as climate disruption continues on its current path.

Natural threats such as weather, predation, and disease all play a role in the function of Moorea's reefs. Though uncommon in Moorea, strong cyclones can create large and powerful waves that crush, break, flatten, and scatter coral fragments all over the sea floor ("Natural Threats to Coral Reefs"). When large portions of reef are eliminated, fast growing algae can out-compete coral, which grows at a much slower rate leading to a shift in the ecosystem from coral to algae ("Natural Threats to Coral Reefs"). An extensive study of Moorea's reef in 2006 by the Gump Research

Station, found that cyclones strong enough to spark this shift have not occurred, and reported that algae populations were normal at the time of the study (Gump Station, 4-5). In 2010 the cyclone Ollie passed the island disrupting the reef around Moorea in varying degrees (MCRLTER, 1). A storm of this magnitude may have altered the reef since the aforementioned study.

The coral population on Moorea is extremely vulnerable to predation by fish, crabs, sea stars, and other marine organisms. Crown of Thorn Starfish (Acanthaster planckii), a species with few natural controls, can damage coral reefs extensively. These organisms are large starfish that can grow up to eighty centimeters and are covered in sharp spines measuring between forty to fifty mm (ReefEd). These sea stars live and prey on corals, which ultimately leads to the destruction of the reef (Davis). Moorea's reefs experienced outbreaks of Crown of Thorn sea stars in the 1970s (Gump Station, 4). In 2007, a Crown of

Thorn Starfish outbreak occurred that significantly reduced the coral cover mostly on the fore edge of the island along with other locations (MCRLTER, 1).

Another naturally occurring threat is Coral diseases. Coral diseases are often the response of the coral to biological stressors such as bacteria and viruses or non-biological stresses such as UV radiation or increased sea surface temperature ("Coral Diseases"). Coral diseases have become more prominent in the last decade, which scientists attribute to the deteriorating water quality associated with human factors ("Coral Diseases"). The diseases lead to widespread coral death. Moorea's reef has experienced a limited amount of coral disease, but a long-term ecological study focused on this topic failed to mention the time period in which they occurred (Gump Station, 4).

There is an abundance of information pertaining to the reefs of Moorea due to the presence of two research stations, one in each of Moorea's most prominent bays. The Gump Station is located in Cook's Bay while Le CROIBE is found on the other side of the island in Oponohu Bay, making Moorea an experimental site for this type of research in French Polynesia. Moorea is far from being an atoll, however this island provides scientists the opportunity to study a young reef as it matures. The research that is being done in Moorea can serve as a template for future research throughout French Polynesia. These stations have extensive relationships with the public of Moorea. They have recently been discussing policies with the government and population to implement some protection, such as the newly designated Marine Protected Areas. Research being done in Moorea today will provide information that will help the Society Islands and other marine communities to better understand their environments. These types of studies, particularly when paired with educational programs, will be able to support conservation initiatives, educate the public, and inform government action to protect such a unique, beautiful, and important environment.

Maintenance and protection of Moorea's coral reef is important for the island's human environment. A trip to Moorea will show that the vast majority of the human population now resides along the shoreline. With a majority of the island remaining relatively untouched and overgrown with vegetation, the human-reef interaction is an important element of human life on the island.

The reef provides protection to populated shorelines because corals buffer the shore from waves, erosion, and property damage (NOAA, Importance of Coral). Coral reefs also help to increase the biodiversity of the ecosystem they are capable of supporting more species per area than any other marine environment (NOAA, Importance of Coral). Preservation of the reef

31

environment could help maintain fishing stocks at a level necessary to sustain the local fishing business. Reefs also have value in the tourism sector.

Recreational diving in coral reefs is a draw for tourists to visit tropical locations like Moorea. The beautiful coastlines associated with coral reefs create an ideal location for hotels, giving Moorea its reputation as a honeymoon destination. The tourism industry provides customers for support businesses that help the local economy. From subsistence fishing to luxury hotels, there are broad economic interests in Moorea's reefs that could bolster the initiative to conserve these fragile environments.

Moorea's physical environment is a landscape in transition. As it moves from high island to coral atoll, the changing dynamics will be monitored and analyzed by two research stations. Moorea's combination of mountains and reef make it a compelling environment to study over time. The pristine condition of both environments and the human capacity to study them has made Moorea a platform of education and research. This knowledge base about the environment feeds a human interest in conserving this beautiful and exciting landscape for the value it possesses to present and future generations.

Our Mo'orea Tour Experience

After leaving the tropical coral paradise of the Tuamotu's, we all were feeling the need to find a location with food and water supplies, a good anchorage, some people to chat to and hopefully a couple waves. The next obvious location was the Windward Society Islands of Tahiti and Moorea. Most cruisers spend a great deal of time in Tahiti; repairing, re supplying, relaxing and really get a feel for the place. Most make a quick stop on Moorea before heading to Bora-Bora and the other Society Islands. We decided to do think the opposite way, head straight to Moorea and then backtrack to Tahiti to do our repairs.

Moorea's distinctive heart shape, deep lagoons and white beaches have long distinguished it as one of the most beautiful islands on earth. Moorea was named after a yellow lizzard which appeared to a high priest in a dream; "Yellow" rea and "Lizzard" moo. Long overlooked as Tahiti's little sister island and a substitute for Bora-Bora, Moorea is closer to the laid back south sea paradise than the other two islands. Moorea has a population of approximately 14 000 and most inhabitants live a quiet relaxed lifestyle. The inner valleys of the island are excellent growing grounds for coconut, pineapple, vanilla, bananas and nearly every tropical fruit imaginable.

Moorea is the remaining southern rim of a giant volcano. Two deep bays (Cook's Bay and Opunohu Bay) formed in the flooded center of the island while the raised core of the volcano, Mt. Rotui, separates the bays with it's impressive shear walls and vegetation draped valleys. In the centre of the island, the shark-tooth shaped Mt. Mouaroa is pierced by a distinctive hole near its summit. According to local tradition, this hole was created when the demigod, Pai, threw his spear from neighbouring Tahiti to prevent the island being carried off by the the god of thieves, Hiro.

Moorea was first discovered by Europeans in 1767 by Captain Samuel Wallis, who named the island "Duke of York Island", before continuing on his way without making landfall. Captain Cook was the first European to make landfall and his visit was brutal. He smashed islander's canoes and burned their homes in response to the islanders not returning a stolen goat. One stolen goat = Burning your house and canoe. Such is the way of the early explorers. Moorea was traditionally a refuge for defeated Tahitian warriors, and many attempts to take control of negihbouring Tahiti where planned and organized on Moorea.

Our stay on Moorea has been nothing short of idylic. Long morning and evening surfs in the numerous reef passes that surround the island, hikes into the mountains to get a visual of the entire island, swimming at the pool of the lovely Sheraton resort (We are currently staying in room 12), and fresh baguettes in the morning. Since much of the coastline of Moorea has been staked out by local plantations, houses or resorts we have been having a hard time finding a beach of beach which isn't constantly cleaned by these ever friendly and conscientious people. Today we are off to another anchorage on the south side, where we hope to find an undisturbed beach to perform another garbage study.

Much of the South Pacific still falls under French rule and the clash of cultures is still evident. It seems the two cultures, the French and the traditional Mooreaian people, are still two very different groups. On many of the islands we have visited the rift between the groups is very evident. When wandering by large groups of local islanders, we get a limited response to "Bonjour" but as soon as we say the equivalent, we get huge smiles. We questioned people about this and apparently the locals prefer not to use French and try to avoid it.

Another example is Pascal. One evening out, getting away from the boat, a single man started chatting to us, and we invited him to join us for a drink. Middle aged, tanned, and could speak the local language, we expected to be able to get some local lowdown from this fellow. Pascal joined us and immediately had a warning for us; "Stay away from the local ladies!". "Hmmmm…. Ok, why?" we asked. Pascal proceeded to tell us all the issues he has had with the local ladies over his 25 years in the Windward Islands (Tahiti and

Moorea). Some of the things he said were completely unforgivable and he truly believed the locals were not the same humans as you and I. They were a inferior species. "So why stay here then, go back to France" we questioned. Then we discover that Pascal has been stationed in the Windward Islands by the French Government to report back on the situation here! With his distorted view, I can only imagine how the reports back to France must read.

The French heavily subsidize French Polynesia and its people. They provide lighting, wharfs, and many many other facilities to the local population, given them a "standard of living" that is definitely beyond what they could manage given what the islands have to offer. However, the French Government's track record with nuclear weapons testing, local land and civil rights is atrocious.

Add all these issues together in the very definition of a tropical paradise and you have a very interesting mix of peoples, ideas and outlooks. These issues make Moorea, Tahiti and French Polynesia very very interesting to visit and learn more about. Take a trip down to the local bookstore or library, grab a book about it and you will both be appalled and intrigued. Then take a vacation, buy a plane ticket and come and see what it is all about.

History

Moorea, like the other Polynesian islands, was populated by navigators who arrived in large double outrigger canoes from Southeast Asia approximately 1000 years ago.

In the 18th Century, Moorea was known as AIMEHO. At the origin of the name change, was the vision a Great Priest had on a "marae" of a beautiful yellow lizzard (i.e. MO'OREA in Tahitian).

Marae are ancient stone or coral pyramid-shaped constructions with several layers, on which sacrifices sometimes took place. The oldest Marae in Moorea is the Afareaitu Marae, it dates back to year 900. You can easily visit the Marae on the road to the mountain viewpoint.

The first Europeans arrived during the 18th century, the Englishman Samuel WALLIS, the Frenchman Antoine de BOUGAINVILLE, and the famous Captain James COOK in 1777.

The Protestant and Catholic missionaries converted the inhabitants who are still regular churchgoers. The French Protectorate was established in 1842 and re-organized in 1848 and 1851.

Since 1984, French Polynesia has a statute of internal self-government, with a Territorial House of Commons, a Government with its President, Oscar Temaru since 2004, replacing Gaston Flosse, who had been leading the country for 20 years.

Geography

Moorea is an island of volcanic origin, situated 12 nautical miles to the Northwest of Tahiti. Total area = 3,2618 acres and 37.3 miles around. Sports lovers can bike around the island in half a day. Mt Tohiea, 3,959ft is the highest mountain. Among the other peaks are the Moua Puta (the mountain with a hole) 2,722ft, the Rotui (between Opunohu and Cook's Bay) 2,624 ft, and the Moua Roa 2,499 ft (called Bali Hai after the American film South Pacific) Moorea's lagoon, together with

Bora Bora's is one of the most beautiful in the Society Islands. It harbors 3 "motus"(small coral islands within the lagoon) and all kinds of water sports can be practiced. Viewed from the sea by boat, Moorea is even more beautiful Moorea's lagoon, together with Bora Bora's is one of the most beautiful in the Society Islands. It harbors 3 "motus"(small coral islands within the lagoon) and all kinds of water sports can be practiced. Viewed from the sea by boat, Moorea is even more beautiful

Climate

The average temperature is 79,9°F, and rarely goes above 89,6°F. The prevailing winds are the easterly trade winds. In winter (june to September) the Maraamu is a cool wind which blows from the southeast. The rainy season extends variably from December to April (alternating sunny and rainy spells).

Economy

Polynesian economy is based on tourism and Tahiti's cultured pearls, the two main resources completed by France's financial funds transfers originated by the nuclear testings that started in the 60's and stopped in 1996. Moorea lives off its agriculture, fishing and tourism. Farming is mainly dedicated to pineapples, vanilla, citrus fruits, a little livestock farming in Opunohu's Bay and the valleys.

Environment

Our coral and mountain ecosystems are fragile. Help us protect them. Use public bins. Respect coral, plants and cultivations. Don't break, collect or pick them up. Thank you.

The "Te Mana o te Moana" organization's mission is about conservation, research, coral rehabilitation and communication related to the Polynesain ecosystem.It is indeed important to help the sensitization to the fragility of our ecosystem.

The PGEM is also a legal way of preserving the lagoon and its fauna

A great variety of tropical fruit, pineapples, grapefruits, bananas, oranges, lemons, papayas, guavas, mangoes, made possible the opening of a fruit juices factory. More than 17,000 inhabitants, essentially Polynesian or "demi" (mixed blood), live on Moorea, scattered all around the island and in the valleys. 48% of the population are under 20. The main employing sectors are fishing, agriculture (mainly pineapple growing) and tourism, but many people go to Tahiti to work every day

Moorea Maritime History and Culture

When Polynesians first arrived at Moorea, they were unable to survive solely on the terrestrial resources and developed a close relationship with the ocean. This relationship shaped early Moorean culture and is still important. The Mooreans required sea-worthy voyaging canoes and navigation methods to travel to other islands. As a population became established on Moorea, boat-building advancements were essential for taking advantage of available fish resources. Polynesians developed many fishing methods to catch the species around Moorea, and fish was a prominent part of their diet. In modern times the ocean continues to be an important resource, for food as well as employment.

Religion

Early Polynesian religion was closely connected to the ocean.In ancient Polynesia, *Tangaroa* was worshiped as the God of the sea and the ocean was viewed as having its own spiritual aura (Elliott, 2004). These beliefs evolved among people who were around the ocean a great deal. Since the arrival of European missionaries in Polynesia, the ocean has had less presence in religious customs. A majority of the current population is Christian and no longer practices the rituals of their ancestors. There remain however, vestiges of the beliefs that the islanders had before European contact.

Many families continue to tend religious sites called *maraes*. Most of these areas are walled in to keep a sort of positive, metaphysical energy from escaping. Some Polynesians consider the ocean to be a similar type of barrier around the islands (D'Alleva, 2011). In the highlands of Moorea, ruins of ancient *maraes* exist as evidence of ancient civilizations. Complex stone gardens with alters at one end were once used as spiritual sites for individual families. The families that held higher social status in the community structure had their *maraes* built at higher altitudes on the island. These sites are no longer used for religious worship. However, they can provide archaeologists with insights into ancient Polynesian life.

The Canoes of Polynesian Immigration

Evidence suggests that Polynesians settled Moorea and the other Society Islands sometime between 700 and 1150 A.D. The ability of ancient Polynesians to migrate to distant islands in the Pacific indicates that they had excellent boat building techniques and navigational abilities. Many different types of canoes existed for various purposes.

There were single hulled canoes, which varied greatly in size. Some would only hold a few people and were used close to shore, possibly for fishing. Other canoes were much bigger and could hold a large number of people and provisions (Oliver 115). The hulls were either made out of one hollowed-out log or multiple pieces of wood bound together. Logs were dug out using adzes, which are like axes with horizontal blades (Finney, 48-49). Boats that were built using multiple logs were sealed off using plant fibers. Composite boats often leaked and water had to be actively removed during voyages (Oliver, 115-116). On islands such as Tahiti and Moorea, single canoes would only have one float for stabilization and it was consistently attached to the left side (Oliver, 116).

Many variations were developed from the basic single-hull design. Polynesians created large double-hulled canoes for traveling long distances in the open ocean. Ancient Polynesians likely migrated from island to island using this type of canoe, carrying many people as well as animals and supplies. In addition, sleeping areas and shelters could be incorporated into the larger boats (Oliver, 116).

Many Polynesian boats were also equipped with sails, which enabled them to travel further distances. Sailboats had one or more fixed masts with booms that attached near the base of the mast and pointed up diagonally towards the stern of the boat. The sails were attached to these frames, starting in a point and getting wider as they went up. A rope would attach the top of the boom to the top of the mast, causing the thinner boom to bow out slightly. This allowed to the sail to form a pocket to catch the wind. On some islands, the triangular sail design that most people are accustomed to seeing on smaller sailboats today was adopted. Sails were essential for Polynesians to take long voyages in large ships (Oliver, 117).

Developing a thorough understanding of ancient Polynesian boats is difficult, due to the lack of surviving physical evidence. When Polynesians stopped making long sea voyages and Europeans brought western influence to the islands, the traditional art of boat building was essentially lost. No complete canoes from early Polynesia were preserved in a way that kept them from decomposing (Oliver, 115). The Polynesian canoes usually did not sink when they filled up with water, but drifted until they hit land (Finny, 43). Because of this, the canoes were not naturally preserved on the ocean floor, but were left to rot wherever they landed.

Historians have done their best to compile scattered bits of information to gain knowledge about the boats the ancient Polynesians used. The most substantial material remains of the ancient watercraft are a large steering paddle and a 17-foot long board found on Huahine Island, which is part of French Polynesia (Finney, 44). Archaeologists estimate that this canoe was likely 25 meters long. The pieces of wood were buried in mud near a stream, which prevented them from decomposing (Oliver, 115). Because of the limited remains, most of the knowledge about Polynesian canoes is derived from written descriptions or drawings.

Some of the best sources of information about Polynesian canoes are accounts from early European sailors who visited the Polynesian islands. Europeans took some measurements of the boats and provided descriptions of them (Oliver, 116). The renowned British navigator and explorer, Captain James Cook, provided a detailed description of Tahitian canoes. He wrote, "Their *Canoes* or *Proes* are built all of them very narrow and some of the largest are twenty to twenty-five meters long; these co[n]sist of several pieces, the bottom is round and made of large logs hollowed out to the thickness of about 3 Inches and may consist of three or four pieces" (Price, 38-39). He goes on to give a full page of descriptions of various types of canoes, including their dimensions.

Accounts such as this and many others give a general idea of how a Polynesian canoe might have looked or been built (Price, 38-39). The only problem is that many of the original voyaging canoes may have already disappeared by the time Europeans arrived. When European explorers first came to Polynesian islands, they did not document finding any boats as large as historians believe some of the early voyaging canoes were. Despite this, sailors' accounts provide a lot of valuable information about traditional Polynesian canoes. The prevalence of information about Polynesian canoes in sailors' journals demonstrates how important canoes were on islands like Moorea.

Within the last century there has been a renewed interest in building ancient-style Polynesian canoes. For many Polynesians, it is significant to connect with their past and continue the traditions of their culture because so much of it has been lost. Historians have also had an interest in recreating ancient boats to answer questions about how the Polynesian islands were settled.

In 1965, David Lewis sailed his modern catamaran, *Rehu Moana*, from Tahiti to Aotearoa, and became one of the first sailors to attempt to retrace the voyage routes that might have been used by the ancient Polynesians. He navigated the entire 2,000 nautical miles using only the navigational tools that may have been available to the Polynesians, and was only slightly off course. Polynesians were able to use stars and the sun to determine direction and their position relative to known landmarks. Lewis's test was an important step because it demonstrated that the

Polynesians could have purposely migrated to various islands (Finney, 35).

Around the same time, Ben Finney, an enthusiastic scholar of Polynesian watercraft, created a replica double-hulled Polynesian sailing canoe named *Nalehia*. He tested it in open water and found that it could sail at a seventy-five-degree angle off of oncoming wind, which would have been an important factor in Polynesian migration. Building on what he had learned from *Nalehia,* Finney began work on a new boat, *Hokule'a,* with a plan to sail from Hawaii to Tahiti and back. It was built based on a generic design, which emulated real Polynesian voyaging canoes. The voyage took place in 1976, and was navigated by Mau Pialug, a traditional navigator from Satawal Island, who used only the stars, sun, and cues from nature to find his way (Kāne, 1998).

The voyage had huge implications both culturally and historically. It demonstrated that ancient Polynesians might well have navigated the seas. It also marked the revival of a part of Polynesian culture that had been lost for a long time. When *Hokule'a* arrived in Tahiti, thousands of people were there to great it. Moorea was likely discovered using a similar canoes and navigation methods. People felt a connection to their ancestors and the voyage had a spiritual meaning for some Polynesians (Kāne, 1998). The first *Hokule'a* voyage inspired the building of many other canoes on various islands. Recently a boat was built on Tahiti, named *O Tahiti Nui Freedom*, which sailed from Tahiti to China.

Some Polynesians have started to make hand-made canoes for their own use. To some extent, traditional boat building lives on in Moorea today (Maamaatuaiatapu). The Atitia Center teaches youth on the island how to restore ancient canoes. Because there are no surviving Moorean canoes, the center has imported a canoe from New Zealand to work on. An expert boat builder from New Zealand has also come to lead the restoration. The design of this boat is vastly different from one that would have been found on Moorea, but people still find it important to carry on some form of Polynesian culture. One of the workers at the center, M. Djelma Maono, admitted that there might be more local interest in the project if they were working on a Moorean Canoe and being taught by a Moorean boat builder.

Modern Boats Used in Moorea

Moorea's current fleet of boats consists mainly of a few common boats, and most of them are designed for fishing. In 2001, fishing was a very profitable enterprise. Gaston Flosse, President of French Polynesia, hoped to boost the fishing economy by developing a fleet of long line fishing boats out of

Tahiti and Moorea. Today, this fleet is made up of sixty-eight boats. However, due to a slump in the fishing industry, not all of these boats are actively being used for fishing (Maamaatuaiatapu).

The long liners that are based in Moorea sell their catch in both Tahiti and their home island. Foreign companies in New Zealand and Australia built some of the boats, but before the slump in the fishing industry, there were four Tahitian companies that, with the help of subsidies from France, built local long liners. Their operation ended when fishing ceased to be as profitable, and the companies stopped receiving support from France in 2004 (Huata, 2011).

Another type of popular fish boat is the Poti Auhopu. These are medium sized fairly sea-worthy boats, with a cabin and an upper deck. Fishermen can take multiple day trips with these boats and travel a good distance from shore on their hunt for fish. Poti Marara are smaller, more basic boats used for day fishing trips in the ocean.

They have a front steering console and are capable of going fast in a seaway. The last variety of fishing boat used in Polynesia is much smaller and is used mostly for fishing in the lagoon. Most are less than five meters, with an outrigger and an outboard motor. This type of boat frequently goes out to the deep areas of the lagoon at night, gigging for the fish attracted by their light.

One watercraft that can be found all over Polynesian is the outrigger canoe, used mostly for recreational activities. The most common sizes are single-man and six-man canoes. They are very narrow and an outrigger on the left side, about a fourth as long as the canoe, keeps it from tipping. The canoes are sleek and powerful boats and are a relative of the more traditional dugout canoes. The modern racing canoes are made out of fiberglass to be light and fast.

They are painted bright colors and well maintained. Each village has its own canoeing center, and every afternoon the locals can be seen out on the water training for various canoe races. Canoe racing is the national sport of French Polynesia. Races include anything for sprints across a bay to grueling inter-island passages. The importance of outrigger canoe racing in modern Polynesian culture is one important connection to traditional maritime culture that is still alive and visible today.

Festivals and Events

There are a number of ocean related events that take place on Moorea. The island hosts an adventure race, which includes a canoe element. There is also a festival each year that begins with a sailing race from Tahiti to Moorea; the three-day festival consists of many events, including canoe racing. Many other surfing, boating, and fishing competitions take place on nearby Tahiti ("Tahiti Festivals and Events").

Fishing in Moorea

The nature of the ocean floor around Moorea requires different fishing practices in the various ocean environments around the island. The reef separates the lagoon from the ocean, creating two types of fisheries, pelagic and reef. Pelagic fish are caught in the ocean outside the reef. Commonly caught and eaten ocean species includes various types of tuna, such as Skipjack, Yellow fin and Albacore, as well as Mahi-Mahi, Wahoo and the occasional Marlin. In Moorea there are over 500 different species of fish living in the lagoon, though not all of them are good to eat. According to Kieitapu Maamaatuaiatapu, the French Polynesian Minister of Fisheries from 2004-2008, you can tell which reef fish were eaten traditionally because when Polynesians don't eat a species of fish, they don't name them. If a fish is nameless, it is probably too small to eat or too difficult to catch. Reef fish are usually much smaller than the pelagic fish and plentiful in the lagoon. These two different fishing environments led to a diversity of fishing techniques.

The historical populations of Moorea took advantage of the abundance of fish and were efficient fishermen. They had many methods for catching and trapping them. One traditional method was groping or catching fish by hand in shallow waters. Using this technique, islanders collected stationary and slow moving creatures, such as mollusks, lobster and fish that were slow enough to be caught by hand. They sometimes even caught octopi using this method (Oliver 87). Poison was also used to gather fish usually made from the ground up seeds of the Barringtonia shrub which was scattered in tidal pools or crevices in coral, stunning the fish and making their collection a simple matter (Oliver, 87).

Fishing implements, such as nets and spears were also part of the traditional fisherman's repertoire. A wide variety of designs were used, from small one-person casting nets to large seines of up to 100 yards. They were usually made of coconut fibers and sunk with rock sinkers. There were also a few of types spears designed to catch different species of fish. Polynesians used long spears that were thrown from the shore or canoes.

They also had a shorter version for jabbing that was used while swimming or wading in the shallows. Spear fishing frequently took place on moonless nights, when fishermen would go out on the reef with torches to attract fish. Using harpoons to catch the pelagic Mahi-Mahi was another traditional fishing style. The harpooner would stand on the bow of a canoe as it pursued the fish, and when they got close enough, throw the harpoon. This method usually resulted in two fish, as Mahi-Mahi mate for life, and travel in pairs.

Various types of angling fishing with hooks and lines were employed by the Polynesians to catch fish. They used fishhooks of all sizes and materials depending on what type of fish they wanted to catch. Some examples are the small hooks made out of shells and bones for fishing in the lagoon and big wooden hooks used for shark fishing. Polynesians were innovative in their fishhook designs. Simple versions of flashers, barbs, and sinkers were all incorporated into traditional Polynesian angling. In traditional island culture, there were some islanders who specialized in fishing. The fishermen lived near the ocean and traded their catch for land-based commodities produced by the in people who lived further up the valley. The multitude of techniques that were developed for catching fish shows how important fish resources were to early Polynesians.

Fishing continues to be an important source of income and protein in Moorea. Modern fishing techniques are similar to traditional methods. Nets, spears, hooks, and line remain important tools of the industry. Moorean fishermen mostly sell their catches in local markets or from stands along the side of the road (Maamaatuaiahutapu).

Modern spear fishermen use more advanced spear guns and slings to stab their prey. It is common to go spear fishing at night, when the fish are sleeping and it is easy to sneak up on them (Maamaatuaiahutapu). Mahi-Mahi are also still caught with a harpoon. The motorized Poti marara is the boat of choice for pelagic harpooning (Maamaatuaiahutapu). Harpoons thrown from the Poti Marara are used to catch Mahi-Mahi as the fish swim through the ocean. This enterprise is usually undertaken solo, and takes skill and knowledge to execute. Fishermen also use hooks and line to catch fish in both lagoon and ocean waters.

Food: Historical and Modern

Historically, Mooreans ate what they could grow or gather from the island and the surrounding ocean. Many of these foods, such as vegetables, fruits, and seafood, were eaten raw or lightly marinated (Oliver, 94). They also had cooking techniques. Preparing a Traditional Polynesian feast involves baking food in an earth oven, known as an Ahima'a. These ovens are made by starting a wood-fire in a pit lined with porous volcanic rocks, which are heated until they are red-hot.

The fire is then removed and the food, usually fish, pork, taro, breadfruit, sweet potatoes and a variety of banana dishes, is placed on the rocks in coconut fronds baskets and buried under banana leaves and sand then left to cook for three to four hours (How to eat...).

Preparing food in this manner is time consuming, and results in a lot of food, so it was not the cooking method used every day.

Modern food in Moorea is a combination of traditional Polynesian food and French food. There is much from the sea to be found in Polynesian cuisine. On average, the population of French Polynesia eats more fish than any other country, about forty-eight kg/person, compared to a world average of sixteen kg/person (Coastal and Marine Ecosystems). The national dish of French Polynesia is Poisson cru, which is raw fish marinated in limejuice, coconut milk and other ingredients. Other popular seafood includes limpets, shrimp, and octopus. This fresh seafood is sold in the markets and from roadside stands. Some less traditional foods eaten in Moorea include rice and Punu Pua'atora, which is the Polynesian equivalent of spam (How to Eat).

Tourism

In addition to providing food for the local communities, the tropical waters that surround Moorea are a tourist attraction. To get to Moorea, tourists have the option of flying or taking a ferry from Tahiti. The ferry voyage costs $10 a person and the jet-powered catamarans take twenty-five to thirty minutes (Moorea: Activities and Sites). The ferry provides a reliable connection between Tahiti and Moorea and allows for locals to commute between the islands on a regular basis. The ferry trip offers scenic views and is a cheaper alternative to flying. This is an important ferry line because it makes it easy for tourists to get to Moorea, and gives the local population access to a job market off the island.

Many jobs in Moorea's tourist industry involve taking people out on the water for various ocean recreations, such as boat trips to the lagoon and fringing reef. The calm shallow waters in the Lagoon around Moorea make for easy snorkeling at many sites. Another popular activity is the lagoon excursions. Local guides take tourists out to uninhabited *motus* for a day of snorkeling and swimming with stingrays and sharks. Dive trips are also popular among tourists visiting Moorea. The underwater features around the island are very dramatic, with many deep canyons and points. According to one tourist website, Moorea has the finest diving in the world (Moorea). Underwater helmet tours are also popular. The boats used for these excursions are usually five-to-ten meter long open motorboats, designed to be a steady platform that can hold a lot of people. Other water craft used by tourists, such as Jet Skis, kayaks, and pedal boats can be seen ion Moorea's lagoon.

Tourists on Moorea also have the choice of venturing out onto the open ocean. Dolphin and whale watching trips are offered and there is a chance of seeing

Humpback whales in the late fall. Bottlenose dolphins and toothed whales are seen near Moorea all year round (Moorea). Deep-sea fishing is another open ocean experience offered in Moorea. The *Moorea Fishing Charters* website says that the fish frequently caught are Black Marlin, Tuna, Wahoo and Mahi-Mahi. The boats used for sports fishing charters are fairly typical thirty-foot modern fiberglass motorboats. These water related aspects of the tourist industry provide jobs for boat-savvy guides as well as all the land-based personnel who organize the trips. This is one of the ways that the ocean continues to provide a livelihood for the people of Moorea.

Sustainability of Moorea's Oceans

The protection of the waters surrounding Moorea is crucial to the lifestyles and livelihoods of Mooreans. Anxiety about overfishing and the environmental degradation of the waters and reefs around Moorea led to the implementation of Marine Protected Areas (MPAs) (Lison). MPAs are management tools implemented with the purpose of protecting fish stocks, biodiversity, and ecological integrity as well as providing economic and social benefits to the surrounding human community (Forrester). They do this by implementing various regulations restricting fishing, anchoring, and diving. The strictest MPAs are "No Take Zones," which protect everything within the boundary of the MPA. The idea behind MPAs is that protecting an area with certain boundaries will have a beneficial effect on not only the localized region, but the regions surrounding it as well.

The *Plan de Gestion de l'Espace* is a comprehensive marine management plan that is being implemented in Moorea by the Polynesian Government. This plan includes the lagoons and waters beyond the reef up to seventy meters deep (Lison). Part of this plan was the development of eight MPAs spread out along Moorea's coast. In 2004 the plan was put into action. Though used widely around the world, there remains to be uncertainty about whether or not these protected areas are having the desired effects on biodiversity and habitat conditions, as they are difficult to regulate (Lison). It is hard to get people who have fished for their dinner right off the beach for their whole lives to stop and there is no one to control or enforce the regulations (Maamaatuaiahutapu).

Moorean people have a close tie to ocean, manifested in their use of the ocean for food and in their early religious beliefs. Advancements in boating and fishing allowed Mooreans obtain a large amount of resources from the ocean efficiently. Historically the ocean has been seen as an inexhaustible resource no matter how many fish were taken from the lagoon and ocean, there were more to take their place. We now acknowledge that this is false and that ocean resources need careful stewardship. If the ocean is going to continue sustaining Polynesia and much of the world, more conscientious practices need to be adopted.

French Impact and Variations in the Human Environment

The South Pacific volcanic island of Moorea was first inhabited over a thousand years ago by peoples from South East Asia (Oliver, 11). It is the second largest and one of the most highly populated islands in the Society archipelago of French Polynesia. Moorea is known as the sister island of Tahiti, the economic hub of French Polynesia (Ile-tropical.fr). Additionally, beautiful coral reefs, white sandy beaches, and luscious vegetation surround the island, creating an exotic tourism locale.

However, the tourism environment and the Moorea that we know today have been developed by several important historical transgressions, most notably the political influence of France in Polynesia. Moorea's relationship with France has shaped the human environment of the island, altering its government, economy, and demographics, and ultimately leading to a potentially unsustainable future for the island.

Before European contact and the subsequent annexation of Tahiti to the French Government, French Polynesia relied on a multi-chief system without any centralized power (Maamaatuaiahutapu). There was a mutual agreement between tribes among the different islands, including Moorea, that there would be no "king" of all of Polynesia, and a stability was "founded upon that agreement" (Maamaatuaiahutapu). If the tribes did not respect this agreement, tribal warfare would ensue.

There was a stratified social system within the different tribes, with the ruling Arii, or chiefs, Toofa, deputy chiefs, Iatoai, officers, Raatira, landowners, Manahune, commoners, Teuteu, servants, and Titi, slaves or prisoners of war (Maamaatuaiahutapu). The fact that each clan had its own Arii and Toofa, and therefore self sovereignty, implies that Moorea probably had just as much political power as tribes in Tahiti, and vice versa.

This political balance between clans and islands ended in the early 1800s, when European influence, most notably the Protestant London Missionary Society, "perverted the internal hegemony of the Pomare clan," (Maamaatuaiahutapu) which was formerly one of the numerous tribes of Tahiti. In short, the Missionary Society helped the Pomare clan gain power over the island in return for their conversion to Christianity.

Although other clans of Moorea and Tahiti tried to protest this centralization of power in the 1820's, they were overpowered by the French implementation of a protectorate in 1842 (Britannica). This caused a brief rebellion by Moorea and Tahiti against the French, which ended in French victory, the compliance of

Queen Pomare IV, and the reestablishment of the protectorate. With the abdication of Pomare V in 1880, both Moorea and Tahiti became colonies of France (Maamaatuaiahutapu).

The Colonial Era lasted until 1945, when a new protectorate was established, giving the power of land management to the queen, although a French governor was still the highest political figure. Over the next sixty years, France made changes to French Polynesia's title, along with small governmental adjustments, but the general power remained with France (Maamaatuaiahutapu). Currently, French Polynesia is considered an Overseas Community, led by a president elected by the Polynesian people, but still ultimately under the jurisdiction of the French legal system and president Nicolas Sarkozy (CIA World Factbook).

Moorea, along with the other 121 islands of French Polynesia, share Papeete as a capital (Poirine, 24). Together with its neighboring island Maioa, Moorea is a commune of Tahiti. A commune is the lowest administrative unit in French government, similar to a town or small city. The mayor of the Moorea-Maioa commune, elected in 2000, is Raymond Van-Banstolaer, a member of the Union for Democracy party (UPLD) (Tunui).

The UPLD is a coalition established by the current president of French Polynesia's Territorial Assembly , Oscar Temaru. The coalition calls for "taui," or change, which implies "a new cultural orientation, away from the French influence and back to the country's Maohi (Indigenous Polynesian) roots, as well as toward a more pan-Pacific perspective" (Gonschor). It does not seek total independence from France, most likely because the Polynesian economy relies on French aid.

The way the government is set up gives almost no power to Moorea, simply because it is less populated and less industrialized than Tahiti. However, one might argue that Moorea should have more political power because of the pristine environment that it is in charge of protecting. Oftentimes, tourists who visit the island may not be concerned about the detrimental impact that they have on the island. Therefore, without the jurisdiction or federal funds to make proper restrictions against pollution and general apathy towards the environment, the reputation of the island's historically untarnished environment will suffer. While Moorea, and on a larger scale French Polynesia, have a relatively stable European-instituted government system, it is arguable whether this system is beneficial or sustainable to the islands in the long term.

Before Europeans arrived, Mooreans exercised a subsistence-based economy (Duane, 2). Small-scale farming and gardening was used to provide food for islanders, which supplemented their diet of fish and other seafood. While the agriculture was small scale, it relied on a highly developed system. Archaeological records from the Opunohu valley on the Northern side of Moorea have noted the remnants of many "agricultural terraces," which were enclosed plots of land for farming (Green, 171). Some of the terraces have walls to prevent flooding in valleys, others have irrigation systems, and several are adapted to only receive rainwater (Green, 171). While the terraces were mostly likely used to grow taro, which arrived in Polynesia around 450 A.D, the same study also found remnants of coconut graters, suggesting that coconut groves were also cultivated (Encyclopedia of the Nations). In addition, the islanders might have cultivated breadfruit and manioc, which are also traditional foods of French Polynesia.

Before European contact, Moorean society was governed by *tabu,* a set of rules chosen by the *Ari'i,* one of which determined who could live where on the island. Because the Ari'i were said to come from the Gods, the sky and the sea were very important to Polynesian society. Archeological ruins of many different *marae* in Moorea have indicated that elevation-wise, both the highest points on the island, the points closest to the heavens, and the lowest points, closest to the sea, were reserved for the Ari'i. For the other classes, the next highest elevations were occupied by other nobles and continued downwards based on class.

Not only did the locations of these marae show the extreme social stratification of the island, but also that Moorea once had a relatively equally distributed population, with islanders living on both the coastline and higher elevations. However, today in Moorea, the majority of islanders live along the coastline, leaving the higher elevations mostly untouched. From this, one might conclude that before Europeans changed the social dynamics of Polynesians, Mooreans used their resources in a more sustainable manner, as they drew from a larger land area. In the future, it is possible that with rising sea levels and a growing population that a coastline will not be able to provide a sustainable lifestyle for Mooreans.

European exploration and subsequent French colonization, starting in the early eighteenth century, changed the island's economy from subsistence-based farming to a cash crop system. As a result of European exploration in Tahiti, a new generation of islanders of mixed Polynesian and European descent arose, and eventually migrated to other islands in Polynesia, particularly Moorea because of its close proximity (Robineau, 289).

This migration increased the population of Moorea and introduced new European agricultural technology and practices to Moorea, in effect changing the scale and dynamics of farming on the island. (Robineau, 291) A higher population meant that more resources were needed, but also that there were more available laborers. Additionally, by the late nineteenth century when this migration was occurring, currency began to flourish over subsistence lifestyles, rendering the islanders' need-based agricultural system obsolete.

The development of plantations ensued, featuring larger plots of land and cash crops determined by the demands of the market (Robineau, 291). The dominant crop was coconut (for coprah), although cotton and sugar cane were also grown, and eventually vanilla and coffee (Robineau, 289). Whereas farms were previously devoted to providing food for the families that owned and worked on them, the plantations formed a hierarchy on the island. This was due to the fact that they were owned by the "Demis," or the islanders of European and Polynesian descent, and managed by local workforces or by sharecropping (Robineau, 291).

This agricultural system lasted until the early 1960s, when France implemented nuclear testing in French Polynesia. While the testing was off of Moruroa and Fangataufa, rather than Moorea, it greatly affected the human environment and essentially shaped the modern economy throughout the territory. First, Faa'a International Airport was opened in 1961 (Doumenge 148).

Not only did that allow for easier transportation between France and Tahiti, but it also opened up the possibility for the implementation of a large-scale tourism industry. Second, the Centre d'Experimentation du Pacifique (CEP) which began to gain momentum in 1963, created many new public works and construction jobs to build infrastructures and supply servicemen for the tests (Doumenge, 148). This led to the transition away from the cash crop hierarchy and towards a France-financed wage-based economy (Robineau, 291). It also lead to a "rural exodus" from peripheral archipelagos to more urbanized centers such as Tahiti (Doumenge, 149). During this time, the amount of farmers and fishermen decreased by forty percent while the wage earning population increased over five fold (Robineau, 291). Agricultural production in all of French Polynesia also decreased from 84% of total production in French Polynesia to 33%, demonstrating this transition as well (Doumenge, 148). Coffee, vanilla, and coconuts, previously the main exports of French Polynesia, decreased by 40% by the mid 1960's (Encyclopedia of the Nations).

In the process of diminishing French Polynesia's agricultural sector by creating more desirable and economically rewarding jobs, CEP profoundly affected French Polynesia's economic dependence on France. With increasing urbanization, demand for consumer goods and external resources greatly increased. This led to a swift and dramatic amplification in the French Polynesian trade deficit. While the value of exports paid for 93% of the value of imports in 1959, by 1902, exports decreased to 56% of imports (Doumenge 149).

With an increasing influx of French money and decreasing exported goods, French public transfers made up 61% of French Polynesians GDP by 1969 (Poirine, 25). In fact, over the nuclear testing period from the 1960s through 1995, the French government became "the single largest employer" in French Polynesia, accounting "for around forty percent of the workforce" (Encyclopedia of the Nations).

During CEP, France actually encouraged and perpetuated this relationship of dependency, because of its need for French Polynesian cooperation with the nuclear testing program. In her article, "Tahiti Intertwined: Ancestral Land, Tourist Postcard, and Nuclear Test Site," Anthropologist Miriam Kahn finds that, "in addition to pumping money into the territory for the testing program, France injected extra funds and goods to encourage local acquiescence, generating a colonial dependency relationship and artificial prosperity." (Kahn, 14)

Though France gave money to bolster the French Polynesian economy, the funds were unequally distributed. According to Kahn, "the French payments, on which the economy depends, are filtered through a system that is controlled by a few families, most of whom are French or Demi. This well-entrenched, privileged class provides built-in assurance that the economic and political system will endure" (Kahn,10). In other words, the money that France was supposedly allocating to French Polynesia was actually handed right back to the French people, rather than giving it to indigenous Polynesians.

By the 1980s, France's influence had profoundly changed the economy. The previously unestablished tertiary sector (trades in goods and services and tourism) accounted for 76% of French Polynesia's GDP (Doumenge, 150). From 1970 to 1980, the GDP from tourists went from one billion French Pacific Francs annually to 8.5 billion annually and the number of tourists visiting the island doubled (Blanchet 18).

Furthermore, as a result of increasing urbanization, 92% of French Polynesian business people resided in Tahiti and Moorea while only 42% of the local population were employed in agriculture and fishing (Blanchet 18). Following the tertiary sector in descending percentage of GDP construction, public works, manufacturing, craft industries, transportation, telecommunication, and finally agriculture made up significant portions of the economy (Doumenge, 150). By 1990, 80% of the islands' food had to be imported (Duane, 3). This marks a huge dependence on outside sources to sustain the changing lifestyles of the population. By 1997, agriculture made up only 4% of GDP and employed 11% of the population (Encyclopedia in the Nations). This situation caused French Polynesia to rely on money from France, as its economy was no longer self-sustainable.

Changes in the economy largely shape the demographic situation in Moorea. The population can be broken up into four ethnic groups: the *maohi* who are indigenous Polynesian, "demis," who are mixed race (usually Polynesian and European), the Chinese, and the Europeans (Blanchet, 1). Today 68% of French Polynesians are *maohi,* 15% are demis, 5% are Chinese, and 12% are European (Doumenge, 145). Of this spread, the majority of the Demis, Chinese, and

Europeans live in the Society Islands Archipelago (Doumenge, 145).

Today Moorea, though considered an outpost of Tahiti, is one of the most populated islands in French Polynesia. The current population of French Polynesia is slightly over a quarter million people, with 75% percent of the population concentrated in Tahiti and Moorea (Poirine, 24).

The population of Moorea tripled between 1971 and 2002, from 5,058 to 14,471, and grew from representing 6% of the combined populaiton of Tahiti and Moorea to 8% (Rafiq). Today the population has grown to 16,000 residents (Gomoorea.com). This is largely the result of increasing urbanization and overpopulation in Papeete.

The location of Moorea, only twelve miles from Tahiti, along with increases in technology and transportation, allow it to function as a suburb of bustling Papeete

(Duane, 3). Many of the business people who work in Papeete commute from the less crowed island of Moorea. Duane explains, "it has been easier to commute downtown on a ferry from Moorea than from the outlying subdivisions of Papeete" (Duane, 3). In addition to the local ferry, a seven-minute flight between the islands makes it a relatively easy commute.

While Moorea doesn't appear to be highly populated during the week due to the large percentage of people working in Tahiti, there are actually a lot of people inhabiting the small coastal strip around the island. Pressures on available land have caused development to start to move further up the river valleys. Ultimately, this growth is not sustainable because eventually the island will become over populated. Moreover, the effects of overpopulation and consequential industrialization can hurt the tourism industry, as it will no longer be the pristine environment desired by eco-tourists who are looking for a remote getaway.

Today in Moorea, tourism, the tertiary sector, fishing, and agriculture account for the majority of Moorea's GDP, with agriculture and fishing only accounting for a small percentage of income (gomoorea.com). While French Polynesia has a higher standard of living than many other island nations, the future of the economy appears to be less certain. Strong protectionism on imports negatively effects foreign trade, and an over-valued French Pacific Franc (as a result of its binding to the Euro) lead to a high cost of living, thereby negatively impacting competitiveness, especially in tourism.

Ultimately, the decisions made by France have put French Polynesia, including Moorea, in a difficult economic position. Their dependence on French aid and the tourism industry to bolster their economy has dramatically decreased their exports and increased their imports, which in the long run could prove to be economically unsustainable. Any hope that the tourism industry might eventually provide an economic alternative to French aid is slim, simply because the money accrued by tourism does not usually go back to the local community. This is because the hotels and other infrastructures that tourists visit when they go to places like French Polynesia are "foreign-owned and managed" (Encyclopedia of the Nations).

Even if tourism was a viable option for Moorea, it has declined since 2000 due to the state of the global economy and the high exchange rate for tourists (Porrin, 29). The combination of these two effects, along with a growing population, does not bode well for the economy in Moorea. Furthermore, with population increasing at a very high rate, urbanization of the island will eventually, if it has not already, surpass the carrying capacity and lead to a greater strain on resources and dependence on external goods. France's historical and current influence in French Polynesia will without doubt continue to shape the human environment of Moorea and all of the French Polynesian islands for years to come.

Culture

Language

Tahiti's official language is French, but most of the Tahitians speak Reo Mao'hi among themselves. English is however spoken in all hotels and most tourist-oriented businesses.

Church Service

Protestant: 80 % of the Society islands population is protestant. The fist temple, in Papetoai was rebuild in 1867 on the remnants of the old one.

Maharepa, Teavaro, Afareaitu, Haapiti and Papetoai, mass on Sundays at 10:00 am.

Catholic: On Sundays, mass at 10:00 am at Pao Pao, 8:00 at Papetoai, 7:30 at Haapiti and saturday at 6:00pm at Afareaitu

Local Art and Craft

Traditional artisanal (arts & crafts), known for its extreme delicacy, keeps developing throughout the islands. Thousands of talented artists make items made of woven material, coconut, pendants, shells and feather, including stone

wood or mother of pearl carvings, not to mention hats and the amazing tifaifai (patchwork).

The items in tapa are part of the most sought after items. Tapa is made from the skillfully worked bark of purau, or other local trees, which in the old days was used for clothing and as support for the many tattoo patterns.

All year round, there are exhibitions-sale to help the promotion of the polynesian handcraft which has managed to «modernize» itself by combining the ancestral art with exceptional creativity of the artist. There you will find a wide choice of original souvenirs.

Sculpture

Carved artifacts, often from the Marquesas Islands, are very much appreciated. Miro or rosewood (among others) are used to carve pots, trays, hair pins or pestles, all finely carved with traditional patterns.

The best-known carved item today is the « Tiki », which highlights Marquesan artistic creation. Polynesians also carve mother-of-pearl shells. You will be amazed by their delicate work. Carved mother-of-pearl takes various forms, it can become a lamp, traditional costumes ornaments or jewelry. Polynesian artists also use volcanic stones, coral and bones.

From the Marquesas to the Australs, not to mention the other archipelagos, sculpture cannot be separated from tattoos. The many motifs found in the art of tattooing are indeed invariably used in sculptures on wood, stone and many other materials (bone, mother of pearl, shark teeth, etc). This more than one thousand year old art finds its inspiration in ancient hist.

Petroglyphs (stones decorated with carved motifs), that can be seen in many valleys, show the treasures of this ancestral art.

Still today, tiki, drums, ceremonial accessories, war clubs or chiefs sticks, rich in geometrical motifs, decorate the Polynesians' daily environment. Woodcarving is the most diversified discipline, but while stone carving is more delicate, it is also very much in demand.

In the area of jewelry, finely chiseled mother of pearl or bone has been developed to respond to new demand.

Shells

The lagoons of Tahiti contain an extraordinary variety of shells. While it is certainly exciting to find them by yourself, do not forget that many species are today protected. You will also find a large choice of carved shells in many shops

The Pareu

Pareo or pareu: in the old days, the pareo was made of tapa, tree bark pounded until a more or less thick layer was obtained. It is decorated with local patterns: hibiscus or tiare flowers. The pareo is an important part of the Polynesians' daily life, as much for men who wear it as a skirt or as shorts, as for women who can tie it in a thousand and one ways.

Tifaifai

Hand sewn bedspreads displaying mostly vegetal patterns. The tifaifai is a traditional wedding present.

Tattoo

his traditional form of expression in our islands, is experiencing a strong revival as an art represented nowadays by talented young artists whose designs are greatly appreciated by both residents and visitors.

Hygiene is no problem as all tattoo artists are regularly checked by the local Health Department.

You will be able to find many books in book shops or boutiques about Polynesian tattoo's history and the many original designs.

Some of them are still practising the traditional tattoo.

The Monoi

«Monoi de Tahiti is the product obtained by macerating Tiare blossoms in refined coconut oil. This oil should be extracted from mature coconuts gathered from Cocos Nucifera trees growing in the coral soil in French Polynesia exclusively. Only «Tiare» flower buds from the Gardenia Tahitensis species are used.»

Coconuts from the Polynesian coral soil, produce a refined first pressed oil which is appreciated by

cosmetic laboratories for its unique silky and light feel.cosmetic laboratories for its unique silky and light feel.

The Tiare flower is an endemic flower from French Polynesia.Symbol of beauty and purity, it has become the emblem of Tahiti. Beyond its symbolic and sensual dimensions, the Tiare flower is one of the most important plants of the Raau Tahiti, the traditional pharmacopoeia of Tahiti. In the preparation of Monoi de Tahiti AO, the flower is used fresh, gathered in the morning, at the bud stage and macerated within a maximum of 24 hours. The maceration in refined coprah oil lasts for a minimum of 10 days during which the beneficial compounds of the flower are extracted. The active oil is then carefully filtered. Beauty care as well as body & mind care, the Monoï is also a sacred oil used in many rituals and ceremonies.Tahitian monoi is now famous all over the world for its universally recognized qualities

Tourism

Top 10 Things to Do in Moorea

You'll fall in love with Moorea from the moment you step off the boat. Perhaps it's because the island resembles the shape of a heart. Known as 'the magical island', Moorea is one of French Polynesia's premier destinations. There's something for everybody here: from scuba diving, to hiking to just plane old beach bumming. I spent one month in this paradise during a six month voyage across the islands of the South Pacific. Here's my personal list of the top things to do in Moorea.

Enjoying The Beautiful Pace of Island Life

Only 30 minutes away from busy Tahiti yet a world away, it's time to remove those watches from your hand and the smartphones from your pocket. Island time knows no constraints. Explore empty roads, empty beaches and night skies littered with millions of stars. Moorea is a place to relax, unwind and appreciate what nature has created.

Visiting The Local Juice Factory

There's juice, and then there's juice. Visit the Moorea Juice Factory and discover how tropical fruits are turned into exotic juices that every Tahitian loves. The factory also doubles as a distillery, producing vanilla cream, Tahitian punch, pineapple wine and even sugar cane liquor. Oh and the best part factory tours end with a never-ending tasting session!

Circling Moorea by Car or Bike

Big enough to comfortably fit everyone yet small enough to comfortably explore, rent a car or hop on a bicycle and circle Moorea's 60-kilometer coastline. Stop along the way to buy some tropical fruit, fresh tuna or an ice cold coconut, and pick a nice spot to savor the beautiful views. You'll pass by cute churches, sleepy fishing villages, azure beaches and locals returning from the bakery with a couple of baguettes. Explore at your own pace and get a real feel for 'island life

Feeding Sharks & Stingrays

Picture this: you see dozens of black shark fins sticking out of the blue lagoon waters, beneath them are the long and spiky tails of stingrays patrolling the shallow sandy floor. Then, you're instructed to step off the boat ladder and go for a swim with these guys! Your mind is telling you that it's against all common sense, but your heart is telling you to just suck it up and take the plunge. Once you hit the water, you'll never forget this surreal experience. Shark and stingray feeding lagoon tours usually include a picnic lunch on a small island in the lagoon as if this day wasn't already special enough!

Experiencing Authentic Tahitian Culture

Exotic, mysterious, beautiful and vivid those are just a few of the adjectives you can use to describe Tahitian culture, The Tiki Village in Moorea is the best way to get an authentic slice of traditional Tahitian life. During the day, you can bring your skills up to par with some ukulele and Tahitian cooking lessons. At night, you'll be pinching yourself as a local legend unfolds in front of your eyes in beautiful song and dance. Oh, and they love playing with fire!

Climbing Up to The Belvedere

Moorea's twin bays carve out its signature heart shape and there's no better place to see this (other than from the air of course) than at the Belvedere Lookout. An absolute must visit spot, the mighty Mount Rotui seems to be within arm's reach, acting as a towering barrier between Opunohu and Cook's bay. Down below is the lush Opunohu Valley, where pineapple is grown in abundance. Get here early in the day or in the late afternoon to avoid the crowds, as this panoramic lookout is super popular.

Getting a Magical View of the Island

Unmarked and unknown, trekking up Magical Mountain on foot or as part of an ATV tour is something that should not be missed in Moorea. From up here, enjoy breathtaking panoramic views stretching from Opunohu Bay all the way to the lagoon motus way out west. If time seemed to tick away slowly on ground level, wait until you get to the summit of Magical Mountain!

Diving with Sharks

You've already fed them and now it's time to dive with them. No visit to Moorea is complete without a bit of scuba diving. Contact Stephane & Diane from Moorea

Blue Diving and exit the reef for some seriously close encounters with massive sharks. You'll see so many that it kind of becomes the norm, that is until you come across a lone sea turtle just snacking away on some coral! Visit the 'diving in Moorea section' in the Moorea Travel Guide and get a discount on your dive.

Exploring Tropical Nature by Foot

Moorea rewards those who get off the beaten track with some serious views. Choose from a number of hikes and get to know the island's natural landscape from up close, and up high. Whether on the hunt for a cascading waterfall or climbing up to a ridge with panoramic views, the hikes in Moorea were among the best in the South Pacific

Relaxing On Beautiful Tropical Beaches

Let's face it, the real reason you come all the way to the remote islands of French Polynesia is to find that perfect beach. So don't forget to pack a few books, your snorkeling gear and pick up some fresh tropical fruit along the way. From long stretches of white sand to secluded hidden beaches Moorea's gorgeous beaches will satisfy any beachcomber's taste.

Things to do in Mo'orea

Let us help you experience the best that Moorea has to offer! If you're looking for fun itinerary ideas, we can provide you with a list of the top sightseeing attractions, as well as helping you to find unmissable activities. Whether you're travelling with your family, planning a romantic trip with your loved one, or visiting on business, we'll make it easy to plan an unforgettable holiday that checks all the boxes.

Activities and Tours
Moorea is crammed with must-see places to visit and things to do. We can help you decide where to stay, and make it a breeze to explore the surrounding areas with our guides on where to go, what to see and when

to see it. No matter how long your stay, it's easy to find places of interest in Moorea to make sure that you enjoy your experience to the fullest and don't miss a thing. Leave the local knowledge to us and leave the hassle behind.

If you're planning a visit, why not check out our handy guides to places of interest in the area? You can browse lists of things to do, learn about the most popular attractions, and get help with planning the details of your trip. Expedia makes it easy for you to check out all the top sights.

Moorea Attractions
Expedia has something for everyone, so whether you're planning to get active on a summer holiday, put a spring in your step with a romantic rendezvous, or pamper yourself with a leisurely winter trip, you'll find plenty of attractions to keep you entertained. In addition to scheduling local tours, booking reservations

and scoring advance event tickets, Expedia makes it easy to book your flight, hotel and rental car in advance, all on one consolidated travel itinerary, making for hassle-free travel and freeing you up to explore the sights of Moorea.

Looking for things to do can be time consuming, but we can take the hassle out of planning your holiday. Whether you're looking to get active in the great outdoors, sample the cuisine or catch up with the vibrant local culture, our guides to Moorea attractions ensure that you'll have a successful trip, whatever the season.

Sports & Activities

There are ample boat excursion companies to take you to great snorkeling spots on the lagoon and for a barbecue on a motu. There's also Jet Skiing, waterskiing, diving, and other underwater adventures, along with parasailing and helicopter rides. The island's green and rugged interior is visited by several safari tours that will include the Belvedere lookout and the nearby marae and a venture to the waterfalls. Most hotels will be able to book excursions and activities and many operators will pick you up at your front door.

Scuba Diving

Bathy's Diving. Its location at the InterContinental Moorea Resort & Spa is a short boat ride from Taotoi Pass, which is a favorite haunt of marine life. There are dives for beginners and experienced divers. PK 28.5 counterclockwise, Coastal road, Moorea, Windward Islands. 56–31–44. www.bathys-diving.com.

Moorea Blue Diving Center. This center calls itself the "shark dive experts." They have 16 different dive sites to choose from. Divers plunge off a deep drop-off and venture out past the reef to the open sea. Moorea Pearl Resort & Spa, PK 3, Coastal road, Moorea,

Windward   Islands.   55–17–04.
www.mooreabluediving.com.

Scuba Piti. This small operator offers 11 different dive sites choices; a single dive costs from 6,100 CFP. Les Tipaniers Hotel, PK 27, Coastal road, Moorea, Windward Islands. 56–20–38. www.scubapiti.com.

Snorkeling

Most lagoon excursion operators will include snorkeling as part of the half- or full-day trip.

Moana Lagoon Safari. Operated by the ubiquitous Albert (who runs many tours on Moorea), these six-hour tours on catamaran or outrigger canoes involve shark and ray feeding as well as snorkeling. Cook's Bay, Moorea, Windward Islands. 55–21–10. www.albert-transport.net.

What to do on Moorea Tours. This company is run by Hiro Kelley, son of the late Hugh Kelley, one of the Bali Hai Boys of Club Bali Hai fame. Having grown up here, he knows all the good places around the island. Club Bali Hai, Cook's Bay, Moorea, Windward Islands. 56–57–66. www.hirotours.com.

Submarine

Aquadisco. This little semisubmersible takes 12 people to out-of-the-way sites in air-conditioned comfort. There's a free pickup service. PK 3, Coastal road, Maharepa, Moorea, Windward Islands. 56–40–90. www.aquadisco.com.

Mer et Montagne Excursions. This hiking company runs underwater tours with aquascopes or glass-bottom boats that skim across the surface of the lagoon to allow passengers to see the coral below. 56–16–48.

Lagoon Excursions

Half- or full-day lagoon trips visit Cook's and Opunohu bays, shark and ray feeding spots, and on day tours only a stop at a motu for swimming, snorkeling, and a picnic.

Moorea Mahana Tours. Moorea Mahana Tours, at the InterContinental Moorea Resort & Spa and also the Hilton Moorea Lagoon Resort & Spa, is a one-stop-shop for lagoon excursions, sunset cruises, Jet Ski rides, and fishing trips. PK 28.5 counterclockwise, Coastal road, Moorea, Windward Islands. 56–20–44.

Parasailing

Mahana parasail. During 10 minutes of pure exhilaration, you'll fly over the two bays and the lagoon, single or tandem. It's owned by the Mahana Wave Runner Jet Ski outfitter. PK 28.5, Coastal road, Hauru Point, Moorea, Windward Islands. 56–20–44.

Quad Biking

Rando Quad/ATV Moorea Tours. These guided two- to three-hour tours on quad bikes (aka, all-terrain vehicles) travel along hidden paths in the interior, to the Belvedere, and other amazing viewing points. Price is 14,000 CFP for one person on board and 2,000 CFP for the second passenger. 56–16–60. www.atvmoorea.com.

Hiking

Moorea is a great island for hiking, but the trails are often hard to find so it's advisable to take an organized hiking tour. However, if you wish to set out on your own, there are several routes including the Three Coconut Trees Pass and the Opunohau Vallep Loop. You can start both of these routes at the Agricultural College (also known as the Lycee Argricole); ask the staff for directions.

Mer et Montagne Excursions. As the French name says, these full-day hikes go to places with fantastic views of the "sea and the mountain." There are hikes in the Opunohu Valley and to the peaks of Rotui and Tohiea. 56–16–48. mreetmontagne@mail.pf.

Tahiti Evasion. This company runs half- and full-day hikes to the Three Coconut Trees Pass, the "balconies" of Mount Rotui, and several archeological sites and long hikes of seven days. PK 20 counterclockwise, Coastal road, Papetoai, Moorea, Windward Islands. 56–48–77. www.tahitievasion.com.

Horseback Riding

Ranch Opunohu Valley. You can saddle up every day (except Monday) for one or two-hour trails in the morning and afternoon. There's a maximum of six people required for rides to take place; the trails wind past pineapple plantations in the lovely Oponohu Valley and provide fantastic mountain vistas. One hour rides are 3,000 CFP and two hours costs 5,000 CFP per person. The owner will pick up from hotels. Belvedere Rd., Moorea, Windward Islands. 56–28–55.

Jet Skiing

Mahana Wave Runner. You can rent out the Jet Skis and go it alone, or go on a guided half-hour or hour-long tour. PK 28.5, Coastal road, Hauru Point, Moorea, Windward Islands. 56–20–44.

Dolphin Watching Tours

Dolphin & Whale-Watching Excursions with Dr. Michael Poole. An adventure, with marine biologist Dr. Poole, is sure to pay off with sightings of spinner dolphins year-round and humpback whales from July to October. PK 3, Coastal road, Maharepa, Moorea, Windward Islands. 56–23–22.

Fishing & Boating

Moorea Fishing Charters. The 29-foot Riviera (with flybridge) is ready to go out every day except in rough weather. It can be hired, with crew, by the hour. A maximum of six people is required. The owner also runs Moorea Jet Ski Tours, offering two hour rides that include string ray and shark feeding and a brief stop near the Moorea Dolphin Centre. 77–02–19. www.moorea-fishing.com

Moorea LocaBoat. You can hire out a small motorboat (no license required) for two, four, or eight hours. Eight hours costs around 13,000 CFP with gas included. To find LocaBoat, wander through Hotel Les Tipaniers to the lagoon and it's just at the right of the hotel beach. PK 26, Coastal road, Moorea, Windward Islands. 78–13–39.

Golf

Moorea Green Pearl Golf Course Polynesia. This 18-hole Jack Nicklaus–designed golf course opened in stages in late 2007. Thirteen holes are located on the seaside of the island road, and five are on the mountainside. It has a driving range on the lake and numerous water traps and well as large bunkers, making it a very technical course appreciated by golfers. It's only the second golf course to be built in French Polynesia (the other is on Tahiti, and was built 35 years ago).Clubs and golf carts can be hired. PK 1.5 Coastal road, Temae, Moorea, Windward Islands. 56–

27–32. www.mooreagolf-resort.com. 9 holes with cart, 12,000 CFP; 18 holes with cart, 21,000 CFP. Daily 7:30am–5.

4WD Safari

Albert Safari Tours. Albert is the island expert and he knows every fascinating place on the hills and the coast. PK 3, Coastal road, Maharepa, Moorea, Windward Islands. 55–21–10. www.albert-transport.net.

Inner Island Safari Tour. You'll be climbing mountains and discovering ancient marae and waterfalls on these trips in eight-seater Land Rovers. PK 3, counter clockwise Coastal road, Maharepa, Moorea, Windward Islands. 56–20–09. www.innerislandsarafi.com.

Biking

Most of the Coastal Road is flat; the best biking is around the two bays Cook's Bay and Opunohu Bay.

Allow a whole day to do the entire 59-km (37-mi) Coastal Road.

Rent a Scooter Centre. There are lots of two-wheel options for rent, including 18-speed mountain bikes. The operators will deliver to your hotel. 71–11–09.

Parasailing

Mahana parasail. During 10 minutes of pure exhilaration, you'll fly over the two bays and the lagoon, single or tandem. It's owned by the Mahana Wave Runner Jet Ski outfitter. PK 28.5, Coastal road, Hauru Point, Moorea, Windward Islands. 56–20–44.

Diving Excursions

Aquablue. Nonswimmers and non-divers alike can enjoy this walk along the seabed, fitted with a diver's helmet. Children from six years old can participate. It's based at the InterContinental Moorea Resort at Hauru Point. InterContinental Moorea Resort & Spa, PK 28.5, counterclockwise, Coastal road, Hauru Point, Moorea, Windward Islands. 56–53–53.

Tour Activities

Snorkeling Tour at Moorea Lagoonarium

Get a remarkable look at the wildlife of Moorea as you go snorkeling in the underwater wonders of the Lagoonarium. A multitude of tropical fish are waiting amid the vibrant coral reef, and a knowledgeable instructor gives you a new, deep insight into the lives of these creatures of the sea.

After a short bus transfer from your hotel to the Vaiare pier on Moorea's east coast, a boat takes you out to the tiny island of Motu Ahi for your visit to the Lagoonarium. Pick up your snorkeling gear and join a qualified instructor to meet communities of surgeonfish, parrot fish, butterfly fish, damselfish, jacks, stingrays, or even blacktip sharks.

Watch the feeding and nourishing of these lively sea animals as you get to know the waters around the island, both in the ocean and from the shallows along the beach. Head back to Moorea after an unforgettable experience with the creatures of the tropics.

Half-Day Belvedere Circle Island Tour by Tahiti Tours

Admire stunning views around Cook bay, Opunohu Bay, and the Belvedere on a guided tour of the island of Mo'orea. This half-day excursion gives you a chance to see the island's spectacular harbors, plantations, and archaeological sites for a comprehensive look at the land and its heritage.

The ride from your hotel gives you a look at the unique contours of the island, including its 2 large bays: Opunohu Bay to the west and Cook's Bay to the east. Make your first stop at a pineapple plantation, get a look out from the Toatea viewpoint, and stop at an archaeological site to discover the land's ancient Polynesian customs.

When you arrive at the Belvedere Lookout, you can enjoy a magnificent view of Mount Rotui standing between Cook Bay and Opunohu Bay. Your guide introduces you to the legends that accompany these majestic sites and the stories of famous navigators who changed the history of Polynesia.

The last leg of your tour takes you to visit the plantations of the Agricultural College. Discover the many varieties of tropical fruit trees and taste the juice and other local products derived from their agricultural plantations before returning to your hotel.

Papeete City Tour & Circle Island Full-Day Tour

Explore the capital city of Papeete in the morning and spend the afternoon exploring Tahiti. Combine city sightseeing tour with a circle island tour, breaking for lunch in Papeete to enjoy some delicious local cuisine.

Begin the tour on foot at a traditional market where Tahitians sell fish, fruits, crafts, and much more. Afterward, head to the Cathedral of Papeete and the Vaima Center, before hopping on a vehicle to discover the Polynesian Institutions. At the end of the trip, visit the Pearl Museum before breaking for lunch.

In the afternoon, visit a variety of sights around the island. See Taharaa Lookout, boasting an amazing panoramic view with Tahiti and Moorea in the background. In the north on the edge of Matavai Bay lies Venus Point, named for the transit of Venus observed by James Cook as he traveled to the island.

Vaipahi Garden displays an amazing selection of endemic plants set in exotic décor. The Grotto Caves form an optical illusion between the ceiling of the caves and the surface of a lake beneath. Finally, Tahiti's best example of Marae or ancient Polynesian temples are Marae Arahurahu, fully restored as an incredible museum

Papeete City Morning Walking Tour

Discover the cultural landmarks and impressive colonial architecture of Papeete, the capital of French Polynesia. Go shopping for local produce and souvenirs in a traditional market, see the palace and garden of the City Hall, and admire rare treasures at the Black Pearl Museum.

The tour begins at Papeete traditional market, where Tahitians sell local products and souvenirs. Admire a wide variety of handcrafted objects as you enjoy the warm atmosphere. Next, visit the Notre Dame Cathedral built in 1875 and restored in 1987 offering a harmonic blend of modern and traditional stained glass.

Visit the Vaima shopping center in the middle of Papeete. Check out local wares and food in the biggest shopping center in Tahiti. Afterward, see the City Hall, a colonial palace and garden inaugurated in 1990, which has since become a symbol of downtown Papeete.

Finally, end the tour by visiting the Black Pearl Museum. Admire a variety of rare pearls, including the world-famous Tahitian Black Pearl. Coming in a variety of beautiful and mysterious colors, they radiate a sublime beauty that reflects their legendary status in pirate tales and mythology.

Half-Day Belvedere Circle Island Tour by Tahiti Tours

Admire stunning views around Cook bay, Opunohu Bay, and the Belvedere on a guided tour of the island of Mo'orea. This half-day excursion gives you a chance to see the island's spectacular harbors, plantations, and archaeological sites for a comprehensive look at the land and its heritage.

The ride from your hotel gives you a look at the unique contours of the island, including its 2 large bays: Opunohu Bay to the west and Cook's Bay to the east. Make your first stop at a pineapple plantation, get a look out from the Toatea viewpoint, and stop at an archaeological site to discover the land's ancient Polynesian customs.

When you arrive at the Belvedere Lookout, you can enjoy a magnificent view of Mount Rotui standing between Cook Bay and Opunohu Bay. Your guide introduces you to the legends that accompany these majestic sites and the stories of famous navigators who changed the history of Polynesia.

The last leg of your tour takes you to visit the plantations of the Agricultural College. Discover the many varieties of tropical fruit trees and taste the juice and other local products derived from their agricultural plantations before returning to your hotel.

Papeete City Tour & Circle Island Full-Day Tour

Explore the capital city of Papeete in the morning and spend the afternoon exploring Tahiti. Combine city sightseeing tour with a circle island tour, breaking for lunch in Papeete to enjoy some delicious local cuisine.

Begin the tour on foot at a traditional market where Tahitians sell fish, fruits, crafts, and much more. Afterward, head to the Cathedral of Papeete and the Vaima Center, before hopping on a vehicle to discover the Polynesian Institutions. At the end of the trip, visit the Pearl Museum before breaking for lunch.

In the afternoon, visit a variety of sights around the island. See Taharaa Lookout, boasting an amazing panoramic view with Tahiti and Moorea in the background. In the north on the edge of Matavai Bay lies Venus Point, named for the transit of Venus observed by James Cook as he traveled to the island.

Vaipahi Garden displays an amazing selection of endemic plants set in exotic décor. The Grotto Caves form an optical illusion between the ceiling of the caves and the surface of a lake beneath. Finally, Tahiti's best example of Marae or ancient Polynesian temples are Marae Arahurahu, fully restored as an incredible museum.

Moorea Island Lagoon Circle Cruise with a Polynesian Picnic

Discover all of Moorea as you make a circle cruise around the island. Stop in several scenic bays, meet dolphins and maybe even whales, check out pristine surfing locations, and swim with stingrays before enjoying a Polynesian picnic and getting free time to snorkel or relax on the beach.

Begin the cruise with stops in both Opunohu Bay and Cook's Bay, both providing gorgeous contrasts between the deep blue waters and the vibrant green of the island. Cruise in the open sea, stopping to meet dolphins and depending on the season maybe even whales.

Check out the Port of Vaiare before continuing on to the lagoon on the other side of the island, where many surfers can be found scouting out the best spots. Make a stop in the blue waters of the lagoon to enjoy snorkeling with sting rays and small blacktip sharks.

At noon, enjoy a picnic lunch on the motu, consisting of mixed salad, barbecue, raw fish, and exotic fruit. Learn to prepare a dish of "raw fish," marinated in lime juice and coconut milk. In addition, witness the traditional coconut husking. After lunch, get the opportunity to snorkel around the motu or relax on the beach.

Sights

Moorea is an easy island to explore by car. The one coastal road is just 61 km (37 mi) long, and the best part of a day is needed to travel the road and stop off at the villages, bays, little churches, and cafés along the way and to travel into the interior to the Belvedere lookout and the marae (ancient temples).

The lagoon and bays can be discovered on organized excursions that may include a picnic lunch on one of the motu at the island's northwest corner. There are also small motorboats for hire for a half or full day, with no license required. You won't find too many tracks of endless white sands on Moorea; however, the top resorts have lovely man-made beaches and the lagoon-side pensions and lodges always have at least a little patch of sand.

Half-day and full-day 4WD tours take in all the sights and some areas inaccessible to motorists, while hiking is a great way to see the pineapple and fruit plantations and lush valleys.

Marae

Just off the Belvedere Road are remains of a few ancient marae. You can just park your car, ATV, or bugster (the preferred mode of transport in these parts) and walk to them. Tetiiroa (sometimes spelled Titiroa and often referred to as the Belvedere marae) has excellent interpretative signs. It's on the edge of a forest, and the "jungle" has taken over: big trees roots have burrowed under the moss-covered stone foundations and trees and vines have sprung up everywhere. A walking track leads through the forest to two smaller marae and the Marae Ahu-o-Mahine with a three-tier altar. A hundred yards or so further along the Belvedere Road are two well-preserved archery platforms, belonging to the Afareaito marae. The sport was considered a sacred game, played by the elite males of the day.

Maharepa

This village is a collection of tourist shops, eateries, pearl stores, a tattoo parlor, and two small shopping centers. The larger Socredo Centre has one of the island's two post offices, a bank, ATMs, and telephones as well as a pastry shop and café. There are several roulottes selling reputedly the best poisson cru on the island. They open for business around 6 pm.

Lagoonarium

This enclosed part of the lagoon near Motu Ahi, off Afareaitu, is home to turtles, rays, and hundreds of fish. A boat takes visitors from Afareaitu at PK 9 (clockwise) on a very short transfer to the island where they can spend all day swimming, snorkeling, learning about marine life, and even nursing baby sharks. There is also an organized tour that includes a dolphin-spotting cruise followed by a few hours on the island. Ask your hotel concierge for tour details.

Jus De Fruits De Moorea

Juice was first pressed at this pineapple processing factory and distillery in 1981. In the early days, four juices pineapple, grapefruit, orange, and apple flowed, but now there are 18 juices and beverages including the famous Tahiti Punch (with 10% alcohol) and various liquors made from vanilla and coconut. The factory floor is off-limits for safety reasons but you can watch a video (in French and English) of the pineapple juicing process. The degustation (tasting) of juices and liquors is free. The gift shop sells drinks as well as honey, tea, crystallized fruits, chocolates, and souvenirs such as T-shirts, and even pearls.

Hauru Point

The point has one long beach that winds in and out of bays and skirts several pensions and hotels for about 5 km (3.1 mi). It's narrow but is wider and sandier in some places than others. Unless you're staying at one of the hotels or pensions, you'll have to walk down narrow laneways between hotel complexes to access it. One such laneway is near the Fare Vai Moana Hotel at around PK 28, counterclockwise.

Hauru Point

Not really a town per se, but still one of the busiest tourist strips, this 5-km (3.1-mi) strip from PK 25 to PK 30 has shops, excursions operators, small hotels, pensions, and restaurants.

Haapiti

The largest village on the remote West Coast is located where the PK 37 counterclockwise and the PK 24 markers meet. Apart from this little honor, it's claim to fame is the impressive twin-towered Catholic Eglise de la Sainte Famille (Church of the Holy Family), fashioned from coral and lime and dating back to the late 19th century. It is framed by lush coconut groves, and jagged mountains rise steeply behind it. The village also has a Protestant church, built in 1916. This white and gray church is distinguished by an olive green steeple and a big clock face. The churches are open for Sunday morning service only. The popular surf break at the Matauvau Pass is about a half-mile off shore.

Cook's Bay

This lovely bay, also known as Paopao Bay, has the most dramatic setting and is best appreciated by standing at its eastern or western shore, or better still, from a boat out in the lagoon. The much-photographed shark-toothed mountain of Mouaroa rises steeply behind it, and Mt. Rotui stands at its western side. There's no real township, just a smattering of shops, restaurants, and small hotels along the northeast corner. The village of Paopao sits at the base (or head) of the bay at PK 9.5; it has a daily market (Mon.–Sat. 6 am–5 pm, Sun. 4:30 am 8 am) selling food and local crafts, and nearby is the Van der Heyde art gallery. The Catholic church of St. Joseph sits on the western shore and is decorated with an old wall fresco of the Angel

Gabriel. For a spiritual experience par excellence, attend the 10 am mass on Sunday morning to hear the hymns and see Tahitians in their Sunday best.

Belvedere

This popular lookout, a few miles inland from Paopao, is the island's highest point accessible by car. From the summit (720 feet [219 meters]) there are commanding views of Opunohu and Cook's bays, Mt. Rotui, surrounding peaks, and the valleys below. The Belvedere road can be accessed at turnoffs from the Coastal Road at the base of both bays.

The road from Opunohu Bay winds through the valley of the same name past grazing horses and lush grassland. The Paopao road (from Cook's Bay) turns off the Coastal Road near the small Paopao village and passes pineapple plantations of the Paopao Valley. The roads meet not far from a collection of ancient marae, and then the journey winds steeply to the top. Use your horn at the corners and bends! There's nothing at the top but the view, save a concrete platform to stand on plus a few chickens and a rooster or two wandering around.

Afareaitu

This village a few miles south of the port of Vaiare is the administrative center and contains the island's mairie (town hall) and a small, early 20th-century church. The village was headquarters of the South Seas Academy in the early 19th century, whose mission was to spread the Protestant faith. Nearby is Marae Umarea, the oldest on the island, dating back to AD 900. The two Afareaitu waterfalls, often just called waterfall 1 and 2, are inland from the village via different dirt roads. You can drive to car parks and take a 20- to 30-minute walk to each of them. Pack a swimsuit as there are rockpools ideal for swimming. Afareaitu also has the island's only hospital.

Temae

It's the name of a town, a beach, and the location of the airport. The kilometer marker system begins here with PK 0. There are three rental car companies at the airport and a tourism information kiosk with brochures. Nearby are a couple of pensions and the five-star Sofitel Moorea Ia Ora Beach Resort.

Teavora & Temae Beaches

These beaches are the best on the East Coast; their names tend to be used interchangeably as they're really one long beach that starts just north of the ferry port and stretches all the way to the airport. The best section is the 1-mile stretch between the airport and the Sofitel Moorea Beach Resort. It can be quite busy on weekends, but especially quiet mid-week or during the low season from January to May. To gain access, look for the public access sign near the Sofitel Moorea Ia Ora Beach Resort. Expert surfers may want to test their skills on the famous Temae surf break but beware of the dangerous reef.

Pihaena

Between Opunohu and Cook's bays, this is more tourist enclave than village, with a collection of pensions (with restaurants) and the Hilton Moorea Lagoon Resort and its restaurants. The Moorea Juice Factory is just a little inland from the coastal road here; bulky Mt. Rotui looms large directly behind.

Papetoai Temple

This temple is the main attraction of little Papetoai and is also known as the Octagonal Church, due to its eight sides. Protestant missionaries constructed it between 1822 and 1827 deliberately on the site of a former marae in an effort to assert the new religion. The buttercup-yellow church with a red roof was rebuilt in the latter part of the 19th century but remains the oldest European building still in use in the South

Pacific. Just one spike-shaped stone remains from the days when it was a marae. The church is often locked, so if you want to see inside, turn up for the Sunday church service. Nearby is the small dock where cruise ship passengers come ashore by tender boats. Craft markets stalls are set up when a cruise ship is in town.

Painapo Beach Paradise
Opunohu Beach

This public beach, about half a mile long, is on the northeast side of Opunohu Bay. It's popular on the weekends with French and Tahitian families, boys playing soccer, and people picnicking under the trees. There are lovely views back to the bay. Dozens of catamarans belonging to the Moorea Sailing School (Ecole de Voile de Moorea) line the shore of one section of the beach. Opunohu Beach is about a mile west of the Hilton Moorea Lagoon Resort and Spa.

Opunohu Bay

This is the westerly of the two outstanding bays on the north side of the island, and is actually the place where Captain James Cook dropped anchor in 1777. It is much less developed than Cook's Bay in terms of tourism and is said to be the locals' favorite for this very reason. Most of the Polynesian scenes from the 1984 movie Bounty, starring Mel Gibson, were filmed in the bay. Big cruise ships moor here, but because there is no port, passengers are taken ashore in tenders.

Opunohu Agricultural College

Called the Lycée Argricole in French, the college comes in view just before you hit the steep part of the road to the Belvedere. Students run free guided tours of the college's vanilla and coffee tree plantations and tropical flower gardens. It's also a pit stop for a refreshing fruit juice or snack and the starting point for three circular hiking trails that can done on your own or with a guide. Ask at the tourist office for a map or guide for hikers. The college has a Web site, but it's in French only.

Motu Beaches

When you book a shark feeding and motu picnic excursion you'll head to either Motu Fareone or Motu Moea, or to one of several small islands in either of the two bays. These are lovely, secluded places and, on occasion, you can travel independently to them. It's best to check with your hotel or pension to find out how to visit a motu.

Moorea Dolphin Center

You can literally kiss and cuddle dolphins here. Three dolphins (ex-performers and retired U.S. Navy dolphins) live in an enclosed section of the lagoon at the InterContinental Moorea Resort and Spa. There are special dolphin encounters tailored for couples, groups, and families involving snorkeling in the lagoon with the creatures, swimming with them while holding their fin (Apnea program), and learning to teach them tricks.

Vaiare

This is likely to be your first view in Moorea and it's a stunning one. Below cloud-swathed, jagged peaks, the ferry port is a hive of activity during the day. It's adjacent to the marina where dozens of catamarans and yachts moor. Europcar and Avis have desks at the port, and L'Truck buses meet each ferry, as do the yellow Moorea Transport minibuses and taxis. There is a stall selling pineapples and fruit, so stock up here.

Toatea Lookout

This is a high point of the coastal road, just a short drive north of the airport. All the transfer minibuses stop here to show visitors their first view of the lagoon and Tahiti in the distance. There's also a great view of the Sofitel resort's overwater bungalows below. It's a wonderful view and everyone gets his or her photo taken here.

Tiki Village

This replica of a traditional Polynesian village, a few miles south of Hauru Point, has been drawing visitors for 14 years. By day there are fishing and pearl-collecting demonstrations, and artisans are at work weaving, carving stone, painting, and tattooing. At night 60 performers put on a spectacular show complete with grass skirts and fire dancing. The audience gets a lesson in pareo (sarong) tying and hip swinging. If you don't want to be dragged up on stage, don't sit in the front. If you buy a ticket to the nightly show, you receive a free day pass to the village. The village is also well known for its Polynesian wedding ceremonies, which must be booked well in advance.

Tiahura

While you won't see this name much, it is the official name for the area on Moorea's northwest corner with the biggest concentration of hotels, restaurants, boutiques, and other shops strung along the main road, or just off it toward the lagoon. Moorea residents like to say there isn't really a main town on the island at all, but Tiahura seems the closest thing to it as far as tourists are concerned. It extends into Hauru Point. The focal point is the Le Petit Village shopping center, a pearl shop, a bank, souvenirs stores, and an Internet café.

Shopping

Many creative people have made Moorea their home, choosing its peaceful environment over bustling Pape'ete. They include painters, sculptors, wood carvers, and tattoo artists, many of whom have studios and galleries. Boutiques sell the famous black pearls and others sell pareos (Tahitian sarongs) and original-design clothing and jewelry.

Tahia Pearls

Former beauty queen Tahia Collins (she was Miss Moorea in 1994) has boutiques near Le Petit Village and at the Moorea Pearl Resort and aboard the Paul Gaugin cruise ship. Free pickup from hotels and cruise ships.

Moorea Pearl Resort & Spa

Albert Dunday, who placed second in French Polynesia's popular tattoo festival a few years ago, is now the resident tattooist at the Moorea Pearl Resort. Using state-of-the-art machinery, he creates traditional-style black ink tattoos.

Moorea Lagoon Spa

Since Hilton took over this resort, the spa, formerly Mandara, has a new name and offers their signature Moorea Forever massage and a choice of two decadent couples' massages and facials using the earth's bounty including coconut milk, tiare flowers, ginger, and the vanilla bean.

Lespa De L'hotel Sofitel Moorea Ia Ora Beach Resort

Here you can escape the world in a papaya cocoon or be revitalized by a hot and cool shell massage, where shells are placed on the body at various pressure points. The refurbished hotel has seven new treatment rooms.

James Samuela's Moorea Tattoo

Traditional tattoo artist James Samuela, who has been practicing for more than 10 years, is one of only seven artists in French Polynesia who still practices the ancient techniques first used by the warriors of the Marquesas Islands. The ban on traditional tattooing (using sterilized wooden and bone implements) was lifted in 2001.

Helene Spa

This is the home of Helene Spa, the only spa concession on the island. Relax in a river bath, be revitalized with a pineapple, papaya, or grapefruit wrap and scrub, and be cleansed under a waterfall shower.

Green Lagoon Moorea Art Gallery

The gallery displays paintings of local artists island and islander scenes sculpture, and photographs. Gallery pieces are also exhibited at the InterContinental Moorea Resort & Spa.

Galerie Van Der Heyde

Galerie Van der Heyde. This gallery displays the work of resident Dutch painter Aad Van der Heyde, who has lived in Moorea for more than 30 years. Other displays include Marquesan wood carvings, shell jewelry, tapa cloth, and other South Seas souvenirs.

Eva Perles

Goldsmith and jeweler Eva Frachon has been working with Tahitian cultured pearls for 18 years. The gallery-store has single pearls and jewelry pieces. Free transfers are available.

Art Marquisien

You'll see artworks and Marquesan artisans at work in this workshop and gallery. The best-known carved item is the "tiki" (a representation of a god); delicate pieces made from mother-of-pearl and bone may be on display at various times.

Nightlife

While Moorea doesn't really rock well into the wee hours, there's more entertainment here than any other island, with the exception of Tahiti itself. Some restaurants have live music singers and bands while the resorts (and some smaller hotels) stage Polynesian dance shows. The Pearl Resort has traditional performances on Wednesday and Friday, and Bali Hai stages its cultural shows on Wednesday as well. It's best to check with individual resorts. The Tiki Village turns on a cultural extravaganza, complete with fire dancing, four nights a week.

Restaurant Rudy's

Owner, Syd Pollock, has been running restaurants and bars in French Polynesia for 40 years. Now his elder son, Rudy, is turning on the fun with live music Tuesday, Friday, and Saturday nights to accompany the good food.

La Plantation De Moorea

The entertainment at this restaurant in Le Petit Village runs from three-piece jazz combos and soul bands to Elvis impersonators and funky DJs at the parties held several times a month.

Other Restauranrs

- ✓ Hotel Kaveka

- ✓ Motu Iti Bar

✓ Tiki Village

Restaurants

Sunset Restaurant

Location and reasonably priced meals are the attraction at this casual restaurant right on the beach at Hauru Point. Lunch dishes include fish burgers, omelets, and toasted sandwiches while pizzas and pastas (all around 1,700 CFP) are served at dinner. There's a menu for kids, too. Try the mahimahi with coconut sauce or the beef tenderloin with green pepper sauce and finish off with flambé bananas or baked coconut tart.

Restaurant Rudy's

Try the legendary parrot fish stuffed with crabmeat, the mussels or ask the owner, Rudy, who's often tending the bar, for his suggestions. Steak lovers have plenty of choices too or they might prefer the stuffed boneless duck with port wine sauce or the lamb. It's a happy place with music. You can't miss it it's an all-white adobe style building on the mountainside of the main road, not far from the Pearl Resort. It offers free hotel transfers.

Le Matiehani Gourmet

This lovely restaurant at the Moorea Pearl Resort is considered one of the best on the island and it's also the most expensive. Chef Pascal Bionaz, who was previously with the Relais & Chateaux Taha'a Island Resort (also in French Polynesia) is said to create "gastromonic delights" and "dream creations." The menu is a three-course degustation, at 9,000 CFP, with five choices of appetizer, seven of main course, and four of dessert. Three of the dishes, including the lobster tournedos, attract an extra supplement (from 600 to 1,000 CFP). You can start with crab tartar on hibiscus and honey jelly, move on to the roasted mahimahi stuffed with lobster with a side of pasta with cuttlefish ink, and finish with Morello cherries soufflé.

The resort offers "reduced taxi fares," which you should inquire about when booking.

La Plantation

Dine on French and Cajun food while listening to a jazz or soul band at this restaurant near Le Petit Village. A favorite dish is slipper lobster (a small relative of the crayfish) served with a vanilla sauce. Crab cakes and Cajun gazpacho spice things up. The decor of all white is plantation style with white cane chairs and tables. The best deals are the two set menus the discovery (4,500 CFP) and the Cajun (5,100 CFP). There are regular party nights with a DJ and dancing into the late hours.

La Licorne D'or

"The Golden Unicorn" is a charming little spot that wouldn't be out of place in a French village. The tables are immaculately set for dinner with fine glassware and apricot colored tablecloths, while lunch is more casual.

The specialty dish is an intriguing mixture of tempura tuna, shrimps, rice, and ginger sauce, while lighter fare includes smoked salmon and crème fraiche and poisson cru "a la Chinois" (Chinese style).

L'ananas Bleu

Breakfast and lunch at "the Blue Pineapple," within the three-star time-share Bali Hai Club, is popular with guests and visitors. The views over Cook's Bay are superb and breakfast treats such as Tahitian donuts (on weekends) and crêpes are legendary. Lunchtime offerings include steak with fries, salads, hamburgers, and poisson cru. On Wednesday nights the restaurant puts on a lavish seafood barbecue (dishes from 1,800 to 3,890 CFP) and a dance performance beginning at 6 pm.

K

Named after the Kahaia tree from which the restaurant's roof and beams are made, this lovely venue is part of the Sofitel Moorea Ia Ora Beach Resort. Just 28 diners sit at chunky tree trunk tables on groovy chairs and wiggle their toes in the sand. Bohemian candelabras grace every table. The fare is a modern take on French cuisine; there are no heavy sauces and the emphasis is on fresh ingredients prepared in a simple way. The prawns are marinated with tandoori spices and the blue fin tuna steak is marinated with soy sauce, honey, and sesame and cooked to taste. Desserts are light with the exception of chocolate dacquoise (a nut meringue) cookie with coconut cream.

Hotel Les Tipaniers

This hotel has two restaurants. Breakfast and lunch are served on the lagoon (where the bar is open until 7 pm daily), and the main restaurant is in a cute thatched bungalow at the hotel's entrance. Lunch choices include pizzas, burgers, salads, and fish, while in the evening it's an a la carte menu where Italian and

French dishes dominate and may include the classic entrecôte (steak) with béarnaise sauce. The poisson du jour (fish of the day) is one of the less expensive options.

Allo Pizza

If you like thin-crusted, wood-fired pizzas then this is definitely the place to come for lunch or dinner. You can eat in or take away. The only concession to the Tahitian palate is the pizza topped with fresh tuna, garlic, and cheese, while there's French influence behind the "five cheese" pizza with Parmesan, mozzarella, goat cheese, Roquefort, and cheddar. There is also a range of salads and a limited dessert menu, including the great chocolate mousse. Wonderful baguettes straight out of the oven cost 200 CFP each.

Lodging Hotels

S.P.I. Hotel Hibiscus

Under new management, this medium-size, budget establishment on the popular Hauru Point strip has neat little beach and garden bungalows and a wing of 11 hotel rooms in the garden. New owners have upgraded the lobby and restaurant and are renovating each of the rooms with new bedding and paintwork and are adding new artwork. Each room is air-conditioned and has a bathroom with hot water and a small corner kitchenette with fridge.

Bungalows are fan-cooled, have a fridge, a wide terrace, and can sleep up to four people. The hotel's beachfront Sunset restaurant is one of the most popular eateries on the Hauru Point strip and serves French, Italian, and local dishes, plus children's menus. Half- and full-board meal plans are available (5,250 and 8,250 CFP, respectively), but if you wish to eat out you can every day of the week as the Hibiscus is near a handful of cafés and restaurants. Le Petit Village is about a half a mile away.

Villa Corallina

This villa should satisfy those who want to "get away from it all." It's on Motu Fareone, a little island minutes off the northwest coast. If you require a bit of action (supermarket, bars, restaurants), take the daily shuttle back to the main island. Four or five people could easily inhabit the spacious 3,000 square feet that include lounge, kitchen, bathroom, bedroom, and a separate master bedroom suite (750 square feet) serviced daily by housekeeping staff.

The villa's decor is unmistakably "South Seas," with bamboo and rattan walls and furniture and tropical print fabrics. Varnished bamboo poles support the kitchen and bathroom. A one-bedroom cottage is located a few hundred feet away in the garden, and this can be rented if the villa is not occupied. Minimum stay is four nights, and three nights at the cottage. Pricing depends on the number of people staying, starting at US$390 (32,672 CFP) per night for the one-bedroom main villa for two people.

Sofitel Moorea Resort

This hotel is on the best beach on the island. Existing bungalows were recently refurbished, and 52 new garden, 15 new beachside, and 19 new overwater bungalows were added. Any room termed "deluxe" is brand-new. The lobby has a minimalist look with an array of furniture from funky chaise longues to '60s-style cane chairs. All bungalows are spacious and uncluttered with king beds draped with romantic nets, positioned to get the best view first thing in the morning. Bed heads are covered with fabric depicting scenes from two of Paul Gaugin's paintings, while bed lamps have golden shades to bathe the rooms in a warm glow. The resort has a lovely "infinity pool" and a gourmet restaurant, K, which seats just 28 diners in eclectic chairs, none of which are the same.

Pension Motu Iti

The family owners of this five-bungalow pension will mix you a cocktail to sip while you read your e-mails (you can toast the lagoon view from the deck). The pension is on the western shore of Cook's Bay and has great mountain views. Each bungalow has a bathroom with hot water, fan, and TV. There's also a 20-bed dormitory, above the hotel lobby area, which shares bathrooms with hot water. It's a cozy little place with a 60-seat restaurant, open from 6 am until 8:30 pm daily, serving all-day snacks such as hamburgers, pizzas, and fresh fish. On Sunday at around noon everyone is welcome to take part in the Ma'a Tahiti (traditional Polynesian meal) cooked in an underground oven over hot coals, known as an ahima'a.

Residence Linareva

This friendly little self-catering pension, started by a Swiss national more than 20 years ago, was recently taken over by Edmee Imfeld, who owned a nearby diving operation for many years. The residence has a pleasant location on a small beach on the western side of the island, near Haapiti. This is the sleepy side of Moorea with few tourist facilities apart from a take-away pizza parlor (Daniel's Pizza) half a mile down the road and a grocery store a short drive away. There are nine accoommodation units called bungalows, suites and villas, which can take varying numbers and are scattered along the beach or in the garden; the two largest ones can accommodate four and seven people.

Each bungalow has rattan walls decorated with island artwork or pareos; a kitchen equipped with stove, fridge, microwave, and coffeemaker; and a bathroom with hot water. All have ceiling fans while a few also have air-conditioning. All bungalows are Wi-Fi ready (free); otherwise, there's access to dial-up Internet (fee) in the lobby. Each bungalow has a small terrace with a floor fashioned from river flagstones. This is the perfect place to have breakfast, which can be delivered by room service (1,550 CFP per person) if you don't want to make your own. The new owners have also introduced a dinner option, which can be served on the hotel's deck in a family-style atmosphere, or couples can have it served to their veranda for a romantic night in.

Robinson's Cove

You'll feel marooned in paradise when you take up residence at this very stylish villa and look across gorgeous Opunohu Bay from your gently swaying hammock. It's on a white sandy beach Robinson's Cove which reputedly was named after a sailor (not Robinson Crusoe) who was aboard one of James Cook's ships when it moored in the bay. The experience will be totally Crusoe as you paddle your canoe to the front door and shower in the outdoor stonewalled bathroom with views across the lagoon.

There are three villas: Bougainville (sleeping 2 people), Wallis (2 to 6 people) and Cook (2 to 8 people), and each has a wonderful deck offering fabulous views of the bay, one to two bedrooms, living room, kitchen, and an array of funky furnishings and amenities: dishwasher, microwave, solar hot-water system, and Wi-Fi. A guide will explain the villa and the island's attractions, while a caretaker lives nearby. There's a five-night minimum stay, and villa pricing depends on the number of of people staying and the season. The Bouganville, however, has the same price year round which is US$1,890 (158,115 CFP) for two people for five nights.

Legends Resort Moorea

This 50-apartment complex, high on the hill overlooking the InterContinental Resort and the lagoon, opened in July 2008. It's a new concept for Moorea and will be interesting to see if hillside self-catering apartments, with no beach access, take off in an island resort where the lagoon reigns supreme. A regular shuttle takes guests to a private island for swimming and snorkeling. The two- and three-bedroom apartments have terraces with hot tubs and views over the lagoon or to the lofty cloud-swathed mountain ranges.

There's a choice of daily or weekly housekeeping (which keeps rates down) and Legends Gourmet, a delicatessen that sells groceries and other items for self-catering and also serves breakfast and lunch by the pool. The onsite restaurant La Villa Des Sens is open Wednesday to Sunday for dinner only. A new onsite spa offers massages and a range of body scrubs.

Moorea Pearl Resort & Spa

Pearl Resorts encompass the best of French Polynesia with regular dance performances and onsite dive centers to get guests into the lagoon as quickly as possible. This little gem of a resort is a short distance from the Maharepa commercial center, near the new golf course, and a 10-minute drive from the airport. There are plenty of activities to enjoy, a gorgeous spa, and even a resident tattoo artist (Herenui Teriitehau) for those guests who want an indelible reminder of their stay.

Accommodations range from rooms (located in a wing) to individual bungalows in the garden, beachfront, and overwater. Eighteen of the garden bungalows have plunge pools. Kids receive a set of beach toys, snorkel gear, life jackets, and a basket of candy. The Matiehani gourmet restaurant is considered one of the best on the island.

Club Bali Hai

This is the last remaining hotel of a handful that were started by the "Bali Hai Boys," three Californians who came to Moorea in the early 1960s to start a vanilla farm. Instead, they ended up running hotels and invented the legendary overwater bungalow concept. The Club is part time-share, part hotel, and it would be hard to find a more spectacular position in Moorea. It sits on the eastern shore of Cook's Bay with a perfect view of the iconic shark-toothed mountain Mt. Mouaroa from almost every angle. There are mountain- and beach-view rooms and beach and overwater bungalows, although the latter are only partially overwater. The five garden rooms have kitchenettes and several are large enough for families.

A grocery store across the road is stocked with a good range of fresh produce. The resort is comfortable without being luxurious and has a very friendly atmosphere. It's virtually a one-stop-shop with a free dance performance on Wednesday night (preceded by a seafood barbecue), its own boat for lagoon excursions and sunset cruises, car rental desk, boutique, weekly crab races, and a sunset talk every day (except Wednesday) given by Muk, one of the two surviving "boys." Gather round over a few drinks as he shares stories of the "good old days" of Moorea and his interesting exploits. The hotel's best rates are available over the Internet.

InterContinental Moorea Resort & Spa

The largest resort on the island appears to have it all choice of garden, beach, or overwater bungalows, spa, Polynesian dancing during the week, a turtle protection center operated in partnership with the government environmental department, a special coral snorkeling park, and three resident dolphins that can be "booked" for personal encounters. A nine-month renovation program added private pools to the 17 garden bungalows and extended the terraces and added a gazebo to all-suites bungalows, in the garden, on the beach and overwater. Also new is a stunning two-level infinity pool.

The resort's location is ideal on the northwest corner of the island near Le Petit Village shopping complex and several Hauru Point restaurants. The overwater bungalows, however, are not completely overwater (the balconies are but the rest is over land). Meals can vary in quality, so don't lock yourself into a meal plan but take advantage of the free pickup services from the many nearby restaurants.

Hotel Les Tipaniers

Location is the draw for this popular budget hotel at Hauru Point. It doesn't have a pool but it has a lovely position on the lagoon and a daytime beach restaurant with fantastic views. There's also an Italian restaurant, near the coastal road, which opens in the evening. Bungalows with fridges are near the beach or in the garden and each can accommodate up to four people, while the superior category have telephones, and 13 bungalows have full kitchens.

The upscale "vanilla bungalow" has a kitchen and a living room. Interiors are bright and airy with tropical style fabrics and cane bed heads and bed bases. Free activities include outrigger canoes and bicycles. Loca Boat, a company that rents out small boats with no license required, is right next door. A smaller sister property Tipaniers Iti is 4 km (2.5 mi) to the east and has three bungalows, each with a kitchen.

La Maison de la Nature

This budget accommodation deep in the Vaianae Valley is designed for folks who love camping and don't mind roughing it. It's a cross between a backpackers' hostel and a guesthouse with half and full-board options. As the name suggests, the house is tucked away in a natural setting, a few miles inland from the PK 21 clockwise marker (near Haapiti). The owners are avid hikers and conduct mountain hikes and photo safaris and run camps for school children during school holidays. There are four rooms with four single beds, one room with six single beds, and one dorm with 24 beds. The four bathrooms (with warm water) are all shared. The "maison" is solar-powered, has a shared kitchen, living room, library, and restaurant.

Hilton Moorea Lagoon Resort & Spa

Opened in 2000, this resort is right in front of Mt. Rotui between Cook's and Opunohu bays. There's a 10-acre lagoon at the doorstep, and free activities include pedal boats, kayaks, and outrigger canoes. Fifty-four overwater bungalows are placed in various distances from the beach on three pontoons and are priced accordingly. Bungalows have hardwood floors and timber shutters and sliding glass doors leading out to terraces; the overwater bungalows have stunning views of jagged mountain ridges.

Bathrooms have deep claw-foot baths and double vanities. Grounds are spacious and the walkway from the lobby to the main restaurant and boutique leads over a lovely pond and waterfall stocked with huge goldfish. There are three restaurants all with water views; in fact the Toata Bar is on a pontoon. It's only opened in the evening and you can dine here on crêpes and keep an eye out for stingrays and reef tip sharks below.

Fenua-Mata'i'oa

If you want something very different and have money to spare, this luxury four-suite residence is a bit like Louis XIV meets Polynesia and it all works wonderfully. Touches run from bohemian to European with chandeliers, four-poster beds, chaise longues, Oriental carpets, upholstered tub chairs, and gilt mirrors, plus typical island decor of rattan and bamboo.

There is a junior suite that can accommodate three, a prestige suite for two people, a royal suite with two bedrooms and two bathrooms and a collection of exotic and slightly erotic art, while the presidential suite is split-level and includes two bedrooms, two bathrooms (one with Jacuzzi), and a small "office" with Wi-Fi–ready computer and printer. The gardens are beautiful and the French owner, Eileen, who has furnished the rooms with pieces she collected in her European travels, provides a very warm welcome. Meals and half-board options are available, together with a weekly Polynesian dance show.

Fare Edith

This family-run accommodation has four bungalows that can sleep three to six people. Two bungalows have two bedrooms each and extra beds in the living room; the other two each have one bedroom and a mezzanine (upper floor) with extra beds. They are equipped with full kitchen, washing machine, living room with TV, and bathroom with hot water. The lagoon setting is perfect and kayaks are provided for exploring this quiet corner of Moorea.

Fare Hamara

Fare Hamara is nestled into the hillside overlooking Opunohu Bay, in the shadow of the shark-toothed Mt. Mouaroa. It has two bedrooms and trundle beds in the living room, making it ideal for six people. It's family friendly with a crib and high chair, washer/dryer, and TV. The villa is owned by an American couple, Bob and Mary Hammar, and bookings are made through their U.S. phone number or by e-mailing them. The minimum stay is five nights and costs US$1,325, (or 111,000 CFP); 10% discounts are given to three-week and monthly rentals.

17106206R00102

Made in the USA
Middletown, DE
26 November 2018